the herb guide

the herb guide

How to Find, Select, Grow, Apply, Dry, Brew and Cook with Nearly 300 Herbs

Sally Ann Berk

Photographs by Zeva Oelbaum

Paperbacks

Published by
Black Dog & Leventhal Publishers, Inc.
151 West 19th Street
New York, NY 10011

Distributed by
Workman Publishing Company
708 Broadway
New York, NY 10003

Many thanks to Mom's Head Gardens in Santa Rosa, California,
for supplying herbs for the photographs.

Many thanks and much love to James G. Wakeman,
without whom this book would not exist.

Manufactured in The United Kingdom

Library of Congress Cataloging-i-Publication Data

Berk, Sally Ann.
[Naturalist's herb guide]
The herb guide: how to find, select, grow, apllyc dry, brew & cook with
nearly 300 herbs / by Sally Ann Berk.

p.cm.
Originally published: Naturalist's herb guide. 1996
ISBN 1-57912-171-3 (pbk.)
2. Herbs. 2.Herb gardening. 3.Cookery(Herbs) 4.Herbs--Utilization I. Title

SB351 H5 B397 2001
635'.7--dc21 2001018417

ISBN: 1-57912-171-3

h g f e d c b a

This book was originally published under the title
The Naturalist's Herb Guide

Cover design by 27.12 design, Ltd., NYC

CONTENTS

INTRODUCTION

Humans have been using herbs for millennia—to treat sickness, to season and preserve food, for decoration and aroma. Archaeologists have discovered fossils of yarrow pollen dating up to 200,000 years ago. Ancient Egyptians used herbs to make cosmetics as well as embalming materials. Medieval doctors used herbs, albeit unsuccessfully, to treat the plague. Medieval and Renaissance courtiers strewed fragrant herbs on the floors of palace receiving rooms to mask human odors and create a pleasant smelling environment. Long ago, before refrigeration and modern preservation techniques, hunters found that rosemary was a natural meat preservative. It was eventually used as a culinary herb as well.

The ancient Greeks and Egyptians had an impressive pharmacology of herbs. It is believed that they had identified and classified over 5,000 herbs for medicinal purposes. At the dawn of the Christian Era, the practice of using herbs was discouraged by the Church. Many herbal healers and "physics" were forced to abandon their practices or go underground or face the consequences. Much of the ancient knowledge was lost, but much was preserved by oral tradition. The job of identifying plants and herbal healing fell to women. The knowledge was passed down from mother to daughter. Much of what we know of herbs today, besides that which has been enhanced by modern research, we know from this oral tradition. We have also learned a great deal about herbs from Eastern medicine, which also dates back over 5,000 years.

Against all odds, the practice of using herbs is one that has endured up to present day. Many people choose to visit herbalists and holistic healers as an alternative to conventional and Western medicine. Scientists are studying medicinal herbs as possible cures and treatments for everything from Lupus to AIDS to migraine prevention.

Herbs also play an important role in every cuisine in the world. Without cumin, curry would just be another stew. Lose the fenugreek, and you have no baba ghanoush, just mashed eggplant. And without epazote, many people would be unable to eat refried beans.

Herbs make a wonderful addition to a garden, whether it's a large outdoor formal garden or simple window box. Since all herbs were originally wild plants, they are relatively easy to grow in most climates. Fresh herbs enhance any recipe. It is very satisfying to pluck some fresh basil from your garden for your pesto, or fresh mint for the finest mint julep. Herb gardens can be cultivated for their fragrance. Many plants, whether in bloom or not, smell wonderful and enhance the experience of sitting in the garden. Growing your own herbs for teas and potpourris is a wonderful way to create homemade gifts and slow down your life in the fast lane.

Each entry contains an herb name, latin name, and one or more common names. The colored icons stand for the following:

MEDICINAL   **COSMETIC**   **CULINARY**   **ORNAMENTAL**

These icons represent ways in which the herbs are used. The terms *annual, perennial* and *biennial* indicate the herbs' seasonality.

This book is a discussion of herbs and their uses, not a direct prescription. Some herbs have been proven to be toxic, but as with any food or additive, different people have varying reactions, allergies, etc. The author and publisher cannot warrant any effects or reactions and are not liable for such.

ACONITE

Aconitum napellus

Monkshood, Black Sea root, wolf's bane, friar's mantle, blue rocket

 PERENNIAL

Aconite is a gardener's favorite ornamental plant, cherished for its blue hooded flowers. It grows well in almost all climates, in partial or direct sunlight, and is widely cultivated in North America. However, it is extremely poisonous. All parts of this plant are deadly, especially the root. If you have children, do not plant aconite in your garden. The leaves can be mistaken for wild parsley. Some homeopaths and Chinese herbalists use very small amounts of aconite to treat Parkinson's disease and rheumatism, but you should never use aconite except as a beautiful ornamental plant.

AGAVE

Agave americana

Century plant, American aloe, maguey, American agave

   PERENNIAL

The agave is a lovely desert plant that blooms only once, after about ten years, and then dies. It is called a century plant for this reason. It flourishes in the hot deserts of North America, and is perfect for a drought-resistant garden. It is a large plant, with thick leaves that can grow as long as six feet, and as wide as eight inches. If the plant flowers at all, it grows a stem from the center of the plant which can grow as tall as

36 feet and eventually develops yellow flowers. It is a very dramatic plant.

The fermented sap is distilled by Native Americans in Mexico and made into a drink called *pulque*. Along with tequila, *pulque* continues to be a favorite Mexican alcoholic beverage.

Agave sap has very soothing properties, and can be used interchangeably with aloe vera on topical wounds and burns.

AGNUS CASTUS

Vitex agnus-castus

Chaste tree, monk's pepper, Indian spice, sage tree, hemp tree, wild pepper

PERENNIAL

Agnus castus is primarily a "woman's" herb, and it has been used for centuries to treat menstrual problems and symptoms of menopause. It naturally stimulates the production of progesterone and may help reduce fibroid tumors. It is readily available in natural-food and vitamin stores, usually in capsule, extract or tincture form. *Vitex* makes a lovely addition to an herb garden. Although it is a southern European native, it grows well in most temperate areas. It needs full sun and sandy, well-drained soil. It gives forth lovely lilac-colored leaves, which are quite aromatic.

AGRIMONY

Agrimonia eupatoria, gryposepala

Common agrimony, cocklebur, sticklewort

      PERENNIAL

Agrimony has been prized by performers over the centuries for its ability to soothe overused vocal cords. Many vocalists still gargle with it before a concert, or drink it as a tea. Agrimony has some astringent qualities, and may alleviate skin eruptions if applied to the skin as a tincture or infusion. However, keep in mind that it will make your skin extremely sensitive to sunlight, so apply sunscreen after using an infusion of agrimony. The tall plants with their spiky yellow flowers add a lovely, subtle accent to any garden. Agrimony grows well almost anywhere, and will flourish in the shade. The soil should be kept moderately dry. It will usually bloom in the summer months.

ALEXANDERS

Smyrnium olusatrum

Black lovage, horse parsley, wild celery

BIENNIAL

Alexanders is primarily a culinary herb and has been used in cooking since ancient times. Although it does have minor medicinal benefits, most agree it belongs in the kitchen. The entire plant is edible. Especially good is blanched stems and flower buds. The seeds can be crushed and used as a condiment. Treat the rest of the plant as you would celery or lovage. Alexanders is high in vitamin C. The seeds were often soaked in wine to create a tonic for scurvy when other sources of vitamin C were not available. It is a lovely garden plant, which originated in western Europe's Mediterranean region. It is cultivated worldwide, and does best in moist soils under full sun. Its flowers are greenish yellow and quite aromatic.

Exotic Java

Ground cardamom is a key ingredient to Turkish coffee.

ALFALFA

Medicago sativa

Buffalo herb, buffalo grass, lucerne

  PERENNIAL

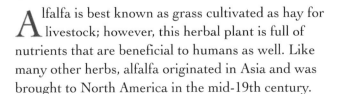

Alfalfa is best known as grass cultivated as hay for livestock; however, this herbal plant is full of nutrients that are beneficial to humans as well. Like many other herbs, alfalfa originated in Asia and was brought to North America in the mid-19th century.

The ancient Arabs were the first to use it as food, and it is often called the "father of all foods." Alfalfa has evolved as one of the premier "health foods," and no self-respecting natural "foodie" would dream of a sandwich or salad without the requisite alfalfa-sprout garnish. Alfalfa is loaded with calcium, magnesium, phosphorus and potassium, as well as all of the known vitamins. Dried alfalfa blended with other herbs, such as chamomile, makes a comforting tea. Caution: Although alfalfa is a nutritional powerhouse, never eat the seeds. They contain a toxic amino acid. All other parts of the plant are safe.

ALLSPICE
Pimenta officinalis

Pimento, Jamaican pepper, clove pepper

PERENNIAL

llspice is one of the most popular culinary herbs. Native to Jamaica and South America, this dried berry of the evergreen pimento tree is called "allspice" because its flavor is reminiscent of a peppery combination of nutmeg, cinnamon and cloves. Allspice is a remarkably versatile herb—it can be used in both sweet and savory cooking. It is also a medicinal herb. Allspice oil, available in most natural-food stores and some pharmacies, is often used to treat toothaches. It should be applied one drop at a time to the affected area. Please note that allspice oil should be used very sparingly. It should never be swallowed—more than a few drops can cause nausea and vomiting. Allspice can be found at any supermarket in berry or ground form. Hot tea made from one teaspoon of powdered allspice is considered to be a digestive aid and may relieve menstrual cramps.

ALMOND

Prunus amygdalus

Sweet almond

     PERENNIAL

Almond trees are beautiful plants that produce some very valuable oil and kernels (nuts). They grow well in temperate climates, but even if you live in a colder part of North America, you can buy organic almonds and sweet-almond oil at your natural-food store. Almond cookies and cakes are perennial favorites. There is evidence that almond oil may help lower your cholesterol. Almond oil also has many cosmetic uses. Sweet-almond oil is a wonderful aromatic treatment by itself for extra-dry skin, and is often incorporated into moisturizers, lotions, facial masks, and soaps.

ALOE

Aloe socratina, Aloe vera, Aloe barabadensis

Moka aloe, turkey aloe, aloe vera, cape

    PERENNIAL

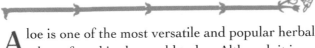

Aloe is one of the most versatile and popular herbal plants found in the world today. Although it is a native of Africa, it has traveled the world over, and today grows in most tropical regions. The most common aloe, the aloe vera makes an interesting, almost carefree houseplant, and has remarkable healing qualities. Aloe has been used by many cultures worldwide for centuries. Ancient Greeks applied the sap, or gel, to wounds and burns—a practice that continues today. Aloe gel on its own is quite soothing to sunburns and irritated skin. It is often mixed with other ingredients to make skin moisturizers, cosmetics, ointments and antiseptic applications. It has been shown to have antiseptic, anesthetic and cellular-restorative properties. A bottle or tube of aloe vera gel in the medicine cabinet has become a fairly common sight as the medical evidence supporting aloe's healing qualities mounts. Some people swear that drinking aloe vera juice is a wonderful internal cleanser, although there is no hard proof to support this. As with most herbs, pregnant or nursing mothers should not ingest aloe in any form, although the gel may be soothing to irritated nursing nipples.

ALSTONIA

Alstonia constricta, Alstonia scholaris

Alstonia Bark, Australian Quinine, Australian Fever Bark

PERENNIAL

There are two species of alstonia trees: *constricta* and *scholaris*. The bark of the tree is used medicinally in the Pacific Rim and India. *Constricta*, which is native to Australia, is used extensively as an Aboriginal folk remedy for fever, chronic diarrhea, dysentery and rheumatism. *Scholaris*, found growing mostly in India, Pakistan and the Philippines, is used for the same purposes, but may also be employed as a treatment for malaria, and is thought to have aphrodisiac qualities. In all cases the bark is powdered and made into a tea. It may be difficult to find these herbs in North America, but more American herbalists are exploring the qualities of alstonia, especially its fever-reducing properties.

AMARANTH

Amaranthus retroflexus, Amaranthus hypochondriacus, Amaranthus tricolor

Red cockscomb, prince's feather, pigweed, tampala, Chinese spinach, hinn choy, love-lies-bleeding

ANNUAL

maranth has a rich history as a food and herb. It was prized by the Aztecs as a grain and grown by the Mayans and Incas as well. Amaranth is native to the tropics, but has recently become more popular as a potherb. Its attractive red flowers keep their color even after the plant dies. European herbalists believed that amaranth stopped bleeding, probably because of the color of the flowers. In fact, amaranth is a very nutritious plant. The leaves may be prepared like spinach and are loaded with iron, calcium, magnesium, lysine and potassium. Amaranth grains have found their way into cereal, breads and other baked goods. Today amaranth is considered a "supergrain," since it provides more protein and minerals than other grains. It is readily available in natural-food stores, and is well worth looking into as a flavorful substitute for conventional grains and flours.

AMERICAN HELLEBORE
Veratrum viride

Hellebore, Indian poke, itchweed, green hellebore, false hellebore

 PERENNIAL

A merican Hellebore is primarily used today as a
hardy ornamental plant. Its history as a medicinal
herb is well documented, mostly through the poison-
deaths that it caused. It is a highly toxic plant, and
should never be used at home under any circumstances. Its rhizome was prepared as an ointment by
Native Americans and early colonists to treat external
injuries, rashes and sores. Later on, it was employed
as a treatment for convulsion, headaches, pneumonia
and just about anything you can imagine. If the patient
didn't die, it sometimes helped these problems. Though
deadly, American Hellebore does contain several alkaloids that can lower blood pressure, slow heart rate,
and stimulate blood flow to the liver and kidneys.
Pharmaceutical companies often use American
Hellebore extract mixed with other chemicals in creat-
ing drugs that treat high blood pressure and hyperten-
sive toxemia in pregnant women. It is also used in very
small amounts by some homeopathic practitioners. In
spite of its deadliness, it can be a hardy and striking
addition to a garden. It is native to North America, and
grows well as far north as Alaska. Its small yellow
flowers will appear in midsummer, and its wide green
leaves are quite unusual and attractive. If you have
children, do not plant this herb.

ANGELICA

Angelica archangelica

Angel root, garden angelica, archangel, American angelica, wild celery

    BIENNIAL

Angelica, the "herb of angels," has a rich history, and a multitude of uses. It has been used as a medicinal, healing herb since pagan times. It was thought to ward off evil spirits and witches, and to

19

Crystallized Angelica

This makes a wonderful holiday treat. The recipe may be doubled.

2 cups angelica roots and young stems (see note)
1/4 cup kosher salt
2 cups boiling water
2 cups sugar
2 cups water
1 tablespoon lemon juice

Place angelica in a glass bowl, and cover with salt and boiling water. Cover bowl loosely with aluminum foil. Let sit for about 24 hours. Drain mixture, peel the roots, and rinse in cold water.

Combine the sugar and water in a saucepan, and cook until mixture begins to thicken. Add angelica and lemon juice. Cook for 20 minutes. Drain and reserve syrup.

Put angelica on a rack in a cool, dry place and let sit for three to four days. Refrigerate the reserved sugar syrup. After three to four days, combine the syrup and the angelica over low heat, and cook until candied. Place on a rack until completely dry. Store in an airtight container for up to 6 months or more. Use candied angelica to decorate cakes and pastries, or eaten alone as an herbal confection.

Note: this recipe may also be used with fresh ginger

prolong life. Angelica water was mistakenly considered to be a cure for the bubonic plague. Native Americans drank angelica tea for strength and as an analgesic. Today, the angelica is still prized for its healing qualities. Angelica tea is often used to aid digestion.
A decoction of boiled angelica roots and seeds can alleviate gastritis, indigestion and flatulence. Dried or

fresh angelica can be found in most natural-food markets. The sweet aroma of angelica is thought to have calming qualities. Add some of the dried herb or oil of angelica to a hot bath for a relaxing soak. Burn some roots and seeds for incense. Add some to homemade potpourri. Many cosmetic companies consider oil of angelica an essential ingredient to shampoos, soaps, creams and perfumes. Fresh angelica leaves add a licoricelike highlight to salads. The stalks can be candied and used to decorate cakes, much in the way one would use candied violets. The roots are also edible and lend a unique flavor to baked goods. They can also be sliced, steamed and served with butter or crème fraîche as an exotic side dish. Angelica is used commercially to flavor liqueurs, gin and vermouth. Angelica grows well just about anywhere, and makes a fragrant addition to any herb garden. It prefers partial shade.

ANISE

Pimpinella anisum

Aniseed, star anise, sweet cumin

ANNUAL

A nise has been used medicinally and culinarily since ancient times. It was probably the first breath freshener, as many Egyptians chewed anise seed to aid digestion, with fresher breath proving to be a beneficial side effect. First and foremost, anise is a culinary herb. It is an essential ingredient in many cuisines, from Scandinavian to Latino, Greek to Southeast Asian. The seeds can be used in sweet or savory dishes. Anise seeds complement any bread recipe calling for seeds. Try baking a rye bread with anise seeds instead of caraway, or combine the two in the dough. Anise is used to flavor liqueurs, most famously anisette and ouzo.

You can make anise-flavored vodka by crushing a teaspoon of anise seeds and letting them steep in a liter of vodka for about three to five days. Strain the vodka, and you have a delicious, naturally flavored vodka, suitable for drinking on its own or adding to mixed drinks. Anise leaves can also be used in salads. Dried anise leaves make a refreshing tea. The small yellow blossoms make a delicate garnish for cocktails and cakes. Anise's intoxicating aroma makes a sweet addition to potpourri. Add dried leaves or crushed seeds. Ancient Romans believed anise flowers kept by the bed would induce sweet dreams. Whether or not this is true, anise is a lovely scent by which to fall asleep. This member of the parsley family is native to the Mediterranean, but is now cultivated worldwide. It looks somewhat like Queen Anne's Lace, with yellow blossoms instead of white. It grows wild throughout North America and can be cultivated in a cook's herb garden. It thrives in full sun. Anise seeds are not used medicinally as much as they used to be, but it is still considered a digestive aid. Some herbalists recommend it to nursing mothers to encourage milk production. Anise tea or an anise infusion may also be taken as a cough remedy.

ANISE HYSSOP

Agastache anethiodora, Agastache foeniculum

Blue giant hyssop, fragrant giant hyssop

PERENNIAL

A nise hyssop is not related to either anise or hyssop, but is a member of the mint family. It is so named because it has a strong licorice aroma and looks like hyssop. It is a beautiful ornamental plant, with gorgeous blue-violet flowers. It is a native of North

America, and grows wild, but is well worth cultivating. It attracts bees and hummingbirds. It prefers full sun but will adapt to partial shade. Anise hyssop makes a delicious iced herb tea. It can also be used as a substitute for anise in any recipe. Native Americans used anise-hyssop root in treatments for lung disorders, but today it is mainly used as an ornamental and culinary herb.

APPLE
Pyrus malus

PERENNIAL

Everyone loves apples. From apple pie to hot cider, it's a quintessential American fruit. Apples, however, are not native to America. They were brought here by European colonists and quickly became acclimated. Today, you will find apple trees growing all over North America. Medicinally, there really is something to the saying "an apple a day keeps the doctor away." Apples are loaded with pectin, which is soluble fiber. High-fiber diets are recommended by doctors to stave off cancer, encourage digestive health, and lower blood cholesterol. Eating apples relieves diarrhea, and it sure is easier to feed your child applesauce than to make her take some chalky-tasting medicine. The only danger from an apple is in the seeds. They contain cyanide. Don't eat apple seeds. If your children love apples, cut the apples into slices and remove the seeds. Don't chew on apple cores, and you'll be fine. Apples are wonderful baked with cinnamon and other sweet spices. You can grow an apple tree in your garden. Start with a sapling of your favorite variety from an organic nursery. If you have a small garden, there are many kinds of dwarf apple trees that bear full-size fruit. Different kinds of apple trees have different requirements, so check with your nursery. Most need good sun and regular watering. If you treat your apple tree well, you'll be rewarded with fragrant apple blossoms in the spring and delicious fruit in the fall.

ARNICA

Arnica montana, Arnica acaulis

Leopard's bane

 PERENNIAL

Arnica is primarily a medicinal herb, used to soothe aches and pains. In ointment or liniment form, it can relax stiff muscles and reduce inflammation of bruises and rheumatism. Arnica ointment should not be applied to any open wounds. It is strictly for topical use, and is toxic if taken internally in any form. You can make your own arnica salve by cooking the flowers in vegetable oil, and applying the cooled ointment to sore areas. Arnica ointment is also available in most natural-food stores and well-stocked pharmacies. If you are growing a medicinal-plant garden, arnica's orange-yellow flowers will add a bright accent to your garden. Arnica grows well in dry soil with full sun.

Do walk on the grass!

Plant German chamomile in your garden, and let your kids trample it. Each step releases a wonderful aroma.

ARSESMART

Polygonum hydropiper

Water pepper, peachwort, plumbago

PERENNIAL

A rsesmart grows wild through most of North America, and is used occasionally as a medicinal herb. Its juice is effective as an analgesic, and is thought by many folk healers to stop bleeding and swelling in external injuries. It is not cultivated, but a trained herbalist will be able to identify the plant in the wild. The plant is also used to produce a beautiful and natural yellow dye.

ARTICHOKE

Cynara scolymus

PERENNIAL

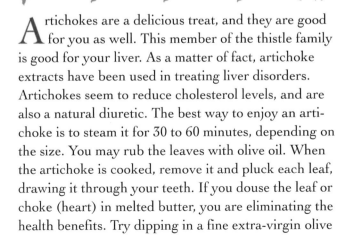

A rtichokes are a delicious treat, and they are good for you as well. This member of the thistle family is good for your liver. As a matter of fact, artichoke extracts have been used in treating liver disorders. Artichokes seem to reduce cholesterol levels, and are also a natural diuretic. The best way to enjoy an artichoke is to steam it for 30 to 60 minutes, depending on the size. You may rub the leaves with olive oil. When the artichoke is cooked, remove it and pluck each leaf, drawing it through your teeth. If you douse the leaf or choke (heart) in melted butter, you are eliminating the health benefits. Try dipping in a fine extra-virgin olive oil instead. Artichokes grow well in moist climates that rarely, if ever, dip below freezing. Most artichokes in the United States come from the central coast of California, where growing conditions are ideal. You can try to grow artichokes in your garden if your climate is similar to the temperate coastal weather of California. If you let the artichoke bloom, you will have a beautiful pink thistle flower.

ASPARAGUS

Asparagus officinalis

Garden asparagus, sparrow grass

    PERENNIAL

Asparagus has been cultivated as a vegetable delicacy for thousands of years. Young tender shoots in April let us know that spring is here. Steamed, or sautéed in butter or olive oil, no one will dispute that asparagus is one of the most sought-after and loved vegetables. It has medicinal properties, and is used as a diuretic. (Anyone who has eaten too much asparagus can tell you that it works!) It is also loaded with fiber, and therefore makes a good laxative. It is a beautiful plant for your vegetable garden. It grows best in sandy soils in moist climates. It will not start producing the vegetable stalk until three years after planting from seed.

ASPARAGUS ROOT

Asparagus cochinchinensis, Asparagus lucidus

Tian Men Dong, shiny asparagus

   PERENNIAL

Asparagus root is used for its diuretic qualities. It may be helpful in treating cystitis and other urinary-tract infections. It is also known as a woman's tonic, and is good for the female reproductive system. Chinese herbalists consider it a valuable tonic that enhances love and compassion. The best way to use asparagus root is by juicing the root, or making a tea from the dried root. The asparagus plant itself is a lovely and delicate addition to any vegetable or herb garden.

ASTRAGALUS

Astragalus membranaceous

Huang Qi

  PERENNIAL

A stragalus is a well-known *qi* tonic —that is, a tonic that increases energy and strengthens the immune system. It is a favorite among Chinese herbalists, and is gaining favor among Western herbalists as well. If you feel sick from the flu, make some chicken soup and add some astragalus root. It will help lessen the severity of your illness. Astragalus is readily available in Chinese-herb stores, as well as most natural-food stores. You will most likely find it in capsule form, or combined with other herbs in herbal tonics. The dried root itself is probably only found at Chinese-herb stores.

AUTUMN CROCUS

Colchicum autumnale

Colchicum, meadow saffron

 PERENNIAL

A utumn crocus is quite poisonous. It is used very sparingly by some herbalists to treat gout, but you should never try to self-medicate with it. It is a beautiful ornamental flower. Native to Europe, it is grown in gardens all over the world. Each plant gives forth a single pinkish-purple flower with six yellow stamens that look much like saffron, but should never be used as a culinary substitute. Colchicum prefers moist and loamy soil, and full to partial sun.

AVENS

Geum urbanum, geum virgianianum

Virginia avens, chocolate root, throatroot

   ANNUAL

The oils found in the roots of avens have an astringent property, which makes it a good digestive aid. It is sometimes used to treat diarrhea and other intestinal disorders, including colitis. It also may be used to reduce nausea associated with an unsettled stomach. Avens flowers in July and August, but the roots, which are best for preparing teas and medicinals, should be collected in May and June.

BALM

Melissa officinalis

Cure-all, sweet balm, honeyplant, dropsy plant, citronele

    PERENNIAL

Balm is a member of the mint family, and has a sweet, lemony aroma. A perennial that is planted in the spring, it is a bushy plant that grows to 20 inches and flowers throughout the summer. When planted in partial shade, it will grow well, without spreading or competing with other plants in your garden. Leaves and shoots can be harvested from June through September, but are best when gathered in the spring.

Balm has been a popular medicinal since ancient times. It was especially valued in the Middle Ages, when it was commonly used as a sedative. Until modern times it was used to treat such a wide variety of ailments that it took the popular name of "cure-all."

Contemporary herbalists still use it to treat hypertension, anxiety and stomach cramps. Since balm is a known muscle relaxant, it is often used to treat menstrual cramps.

Lemon-balm tea has long been popular in Europe, especially in France. It is only with our recent taste for herbal teas that lemon balm has become a common brew in this country.

BALM OF GILEAD

Populus candicum, Populus balsamifera, Populus deltoides, Populus tacamahaca

Balsam poplar, hackmatack, tacamahac, Carolina poplar

 PERENNIAL

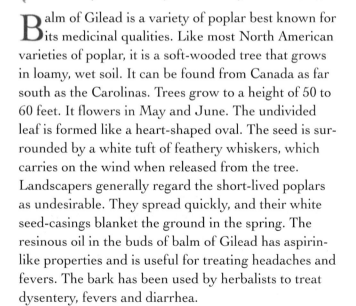

Balm of Gilead is a variety of poplar best known for its medicinal qualities. Like most North American varieties of poplar, it is a soft-wooded tree that grows in loamy, wet soil. It can be found from Canada as far south as the Carolinas. Trees grow to a height of 50 to 60 feet. It flowers in May and June. The undivided leaf is formed like a heart-shaped oval. The seed is surrounded by a white tuft of feathery whiskers, which carries on the wind when released from the tree. Landscapers generally regard the short-lived poplars as undesirable. They spread quickly, and their white seed-casings blanket the ground in the spring. The resinous oil in the buds of balm of Gilead has aspirin-like properties and is useful for treating headaches and fevers. The bark has been used by herbalists to treat dysentery, fevers and diarrhea.

BALMONY

Chelone glabra

Turtlehead, shellflower, bitter herb, rheum weed, snake-mouth, hummingbird tree

  PERENNIAL

This beautiful swamp plant has long been used in American folk medicine to treat intestinal problems. It is believed to be an appetite stimulant, and some herbalists prescribe the dried plant in an infusion to treat anorexia. There have been no studies to back up any of these medicinal claims. It is an odorless, but attractive, flowering plant. Its white flowers resemble turtleheads. It is a wild plant that grows in swampy areas just about everywhere in North America.

BALSAM FIR

Abies balsamea

Christmas tree

  PERENNIAL

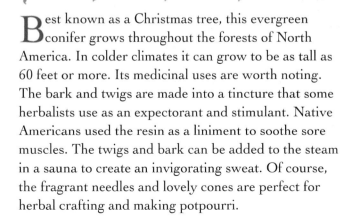

Best known as a Christmas tree, this evergreen conifer grows throughout the forests of North America. In colder climates it can grow to be as tall as 60 feet or more. Its medicinal uses are worth noting. The bark and twigs are made into a tincture that some herbalists use as an expectorant and stimulant. Native Americans used the resin as a liniment to soothe sore muscles. The twigs and bark can be added to the steam in a sauna to create an invigorating sweat. Of course, the fragrant needles and lovely cones are perfect for herbal crafting and making potpourri.

BARBERRY

Berberis vulgaris, Berberis candensis

Pipperidge bush, jaundice berry, holy thorn, gouan

     PERENNIAL

Barberry tea can be one of the best ways to treat a sore throat. It has antibiotic qualities that make it a valuable herb for treating flu, diarrhea and bladder infections. Many people drink barberry tea to detoxify the liver after a night on the town. But barberry is a very powerful herb, and should not be used as a home remedy. It is best to consult a qualified herbalist before self-medicating. In too large a dose, barberry can cause nausea, vomiting and a rapid drop in blood pressure. It is very bitter. An herbalist will most likely recommend barberry mixed with a sweeter, palatable herb. Barberry root is also used to make yellow dyes. The barberry bush is an easy plant to grow. It originated in Europe and parts of Asia, but is found in many gardens worldwide. In the summer it gives forth lovely yellow blossoms, and is self-pollinating.

BASIL

Ocimum spp.

Sweet basil, anise basil, dark opal purple basil, lemon basil, fine-leaf tall basil, fine-leaf bush basil

      ANNUAL

Basil may be the world's favorite herb. It is found in just about every culture's cuisine; it is easy to grow, smells divine, and tastes even better. It is used in many cultures' cuisines. There are several different types of basil, and almost all of them can be used in cooking. Sweet basil is the most popular variety (*O. basilicum*), and is easily cultivated in kitchen herb gardens. It is a good herb to have handy. Dried basil simply doesn't taste anything like the fresh herb. Plant it from seed in the spring. It will keep you in fragrant basil pleasure until the first frost. Basil is the key ingredient in classic pesto. Fresh leaves and flowers can be tossed sparingly in salad. Fresh mozzarella sliced with vine-ripe tomatoes and fresh basil, drizzled with extra-virgin olive oil, makes a marvelous appetizer, or a light salad. Use it to make a wonderful focaccia. The best basil to grow for vinegars is lemon basil (*O. Americanum*). Holy basil (*O. sanctum*) is considered a holy plant by the Hindus and is largely planted as an ornamental. Basil's essential oils are used in the perfume industry, and are often found in commercial hair treatments. If you do not have a garden, but still want to grow fresh basil, it is a wonderful potherb for your windowsill. Look for bush basil (*O. minimum*) for an indoor garden. It is a smaller plant with equally delicious flavor and can survive indoors in a sunny, warm pot throughout the winter. Herbalists use camphor basil (*O. kilimandscharicum*) as a mild sedative and as a treatment for stomach cramps, but camphor basil is not a culinary basil.

BAY LAUREL

Laurus nobilis

Bay leaf, laurel, sweet bay

PERENNIAL

If you're lucky enough to live in a temperate climate, and you can incorporate one or two bay trees into your landscaping, you will always have fresh, aromatic bay leaves for your kitchen. This Mediterranean ever-

green grows to a height of 10 to 20 feet and bears the
thick, shiny, deep green leaves that are indispensable to
so many culinary traditions. In ancient times bay had
not only culinary and medicinal uses, but symbolic uses
as well. The laureate, symbolic of victory and valor,
was made from the leaves and branches of the bay tree.
The many different cultures that have found medicinal
uses for bay over the millennia have ascribed dozens of
healing properties to it. Almost all of these are spuri-
ous, although a bay-leaf poultice does have a mildly
effective antibacterial action. Bay's true value is in the
kitchen. Even the most amateur chef knows some of
the many uses for this aromatic leaf. It will add its

uniquely sweet flavor to any dish that requires simmering. It is a potent cooking herb; a single leaf or half a leaf is often all you will need for a good-size stew or marinade. Even after a half hour of stewing, the bay leaf is still releasing flavor to a soup. Bay leaves are also commonly called for in many pickling recipes. Bay branches make an excellent skeletal base for just about any herbal craft, and the deep green of the leaves will mix well with most crafting herbs.

If you live in a Northern state and you would like to cultivate your own bay, you would be wise to do as the Europeans do: Pot your sapling in a half-barrel on castors. Bring the tree indoors for the harsher winter months, and give it as much sunlight and humidity as possible. A potted tree will grow to no more than six or eight feet, and will always be manageable.

BAYBERRY

Myrica cerifera

Candle berry, wax myrtle, tallow shrub, wax berry

     PERENNIAL

For centuries the powdered bark of the bayberry tree has been used in decoctions to reduce fever and treat severe cases of diarrhea. It may be a useful liver tonic as well. It is used as a poultice to soothe varicose veins. This North American native tree flourishes in more temperate areas. It does well in full sun and peety soil, but will grow in sandy soil as well. Its leaves produce a fragrant resin, which is used in candlemaking. The yellow flowers produce a fruit, which is not edible, but is used in candlemaking, too.

BELLADONNA

Belladonna scopula, Atropa belladonna

Deadly nightshade, dwale

 PERENNIAL

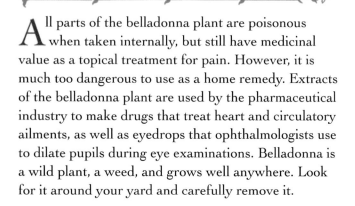

All parts of the belladonna plant are poisonous when taken internally, but still have medicinal value as a topical treatment for pain. However, it is much too dangerous to use as a home remedy. Extracts of the belladonna plant are used by the pharmaceutical industry to make drugs that treat heart and circulatory ailments, as well as eyedrops that ophthalmologists use to dilate pupils during eye examinations. Belladonna is a wild plant, a weed, and grows well anywhere. Look for it around your yard and carefully remove it.

BERGAMOT
Monarda didyma, Monarda fistulosa

Adam, alba, blue stocking, Cambridge scarlet, Croftway pink, mahogany, Melissa, pale ponticum, pillar box, snow maiden, wild bergamot, bee balm, Oswego tea

   PERENNIAL

Bergamot is a widely cultivated ornamental herb, prized mainly for its beauty and citrus-orange fragrance. Red bergamot is the most fragrant of all varieties. It is a Native American plant, and was used by the Oswego tribe as a medicinal stimulant. When the early European Americans were protesting the British tax on tea, many households used "Oswego tea" instead of imported Indian tea. The tea is delicious, and will soothe nausea. The essential oil is used in making perfume, and in some shampoos.

BETONY
Stachys officinalis

Bishopswort, wood betony

   PERENNIAL

Betony is a single-stem perennial, which makes a beautiful addition to an ornamental garden. The red-violet, trumpet-shaped flowers are clustered at the top of the stem and appear again at the leaf axles. Originally native to Europe, betony grows easily in a variety of conditions, in full and partial sun. In the past betony was valued for having dozens of medicinal applications. Contemporary herbalists recognize little more than its astringent quality, which is useful for treating a sore throat. Betony can be gathered anytime, but for making tea it is best cut before it flowers in the spring. Look for it in your natural-food store or farmers' market.

BILBERRY
Vaccinium myrtillus

Huckleberry, hurtleberry, whortleberry

   PERENNIAL

Bilberry is a valuable medicinal herb and a delicious culinary one. It is a native European cousin to the blueberry, and its berries can be used anywhere one would use blueberries. It makes a delicious jam, and flavors certain liqueurs. The berries are a good source of vitamins A and C, as well as pectin. They have been used in the past to treat diarrhea and nausea. Bilberry extract is used to combat myopia and improve night vision. You will find bilberry in capsule form at your natural-food stores. Although native to Europe, bilberry has been cultivated successfully in North America. It makes a colorful addition to an ornamental garden or arbor. The plant continues to blossom long into the fall, giving forth pale greenish-pink flowers. It needs damp soil and partial sun.

Herbs Make History!
Bilberry improves night vision. During World War II, British Royal Air Force pilots were given bilberry jam as part of their standard rations to help them see during nighttime bombing raids.

BIRCH

Betula alba, Betula papyrifer, Betula lenta,
Betula nigra

White birch, paper birch, canoe birch, sweet birch, river birch, black birch, silver birch

PERENNIAL

This ancient and attractive tree grows worldwide in a variety of climates. It flowers in more temperate zones, and its leaves turn brilliant colors in the fall.

Native Americans used the birch as a medicine and food. They used the sap to make syrup and teas. A tea made from the bark and twigs was used to treat many digestive disorders. Today the graceful birch is primarily an ornamental tree.

BISTORT

Polygonum bistorta

Osterick, Easter Mangiant, adderwort, oderwort, snakeweed

   PERENNIAL

Bistort, native to many parts of northern Europe, grows both wild and in cultivation. Its leaves and shoots are still used in herb pudding, a traditional English Easter dish. The plant grows well in moist environments, in shade or sunlight, and is easy to cultivate. It is an attractive plant, which will bloom twice in one season—in late spring and again in early fall. The flowers are a striking salmon color. It has been used medicinally for centuries. It contains a good deal of tannin. The leaves were often used as disinfecting poultices, but it is the root that is the primary medicinal part. A tea made from powdered bistort root is used to treat diarrhea and other bowel problems. Its astringent quality makes it a healing mouthwash for sore gums. Bistort is not often found in North America, but some mail-order companies may be able to supply you with the dried root.

Enhance the Flavor of Dried Herbs

To bring out the flavor of dried herbs, steep them for about ten minutes in a liquid that will be used in the recipe.

BLACK COHOSH

Cimicifuga racemosa

Bugbane, rattleroot, squawroot, snakeroot, black snakeroot

PERENNIAL

Black cohosh is a traditional Native American remedy for problems with the female reproductive system. It is a muscle relaxer, and is still used by herbalists, alone or in conjunction with other herbs such as chamomile, to treat menstrual cramps, labor pains and anxiety. There is also evidence that it can bring on a delayed period. Black cohosh is a very powerful herb. It should never be used during pregnancy, since it will almost certainly cause miscarriage. Even if you're not pregnant, it is best to check with your doctor, or a qualified herbalist, before you try black cohosh for menstrual cramps. Black cohosh makes a striking plant for your herb garden. Its single stem can grow as tall as eight feet, and its flowers are small, white and delicate. This plant is native to North America and can be found from Canada to Texas. It grows well in the shade.

BLACK CUMIN

Nigella sativa

Nutmeg flower, Roman coriander, fennel flower

ANNUAL

Black cumin is a terrific kitchen-garden herb. It has lacy foliage and lovely blue flowers. Its pods contain seeds that, when dried, may be substituted for the spice cumin (*cumin cyminum*). It is much easier to grow and thrives in full sun. Black cumin has a stronger and more fennellike flavor than regular cumin, so be sure to taste it before you substitute. The amount you use may differ.

BLACK HAW
Viburnum prunifolium

Viburnum, sweet haw, stagbush, sheepberry, cramp bark, American sloe, sweet viburnum, slave owner's herb

PERENNIAL

Black-haw bark is a traditional Native American remedy for gynecological problems. It contains a uterine relaxant, and is used to alleviate menstrual cramps. Black haw also contains salicin, an aspirin-related substance, which may also contribute to its analgesic properties. Black haw was discovered by slave owners in the South. They raped their women slaves and then forced the then-pregnant women to partake of the herb. Sometimes it was fed to them surreptitiously, to insure that the women did not miscarry. A woman slave was considered a "breeder," and any child born to the woman would automatically become property of the white owner. The only thing these women could do to silently protest this treatment was to abort their own child by eating cotton root. Black haw is no longer used to prevent miscarriage. The salicin can contribute to birth defects, so it should never be used by pregnant women. If you want to grow this dubious American native, it will thrive as a small tree in the southern parts of North America. In other parts it will grow as a bush or shrub. It grows best in full sun, and its flowers are large, white and showy. It will tolerate almost any kind of soil, as long as it gets plenty of moisture.

BLACK HELLEBORE

Helleborus niger

Christmas rose, Indian poke, itchweed

 PERENNIAL

This highly poisonous plant is widely cultivated in ornamental gardens for its striking rose-colored flowers. It blooms in the winter, thus the name Christmas rose. It is a native of southern Europe, but has been found growing wild as far north as the Swiss Alps. It is not a difficult plant to grow. Historically, black hellebore was used for medicinal purposes by doctors who should have known better. Some believed it was a cure for insanity, night blindness, dropsy and delayed menstruation. None of these claims are supported by research, and this plant should never be ingested for any reason. It is toxic.

BLACKBERRY

Rubus villosus, Rubus fruticosus

Brambleberry, dewberry, goutberry

   PERENNIAL

Along with raspberries and boysenberries, this thorny shrub belongs to a family that includes over 200 species of berry bushes. Most of these are characterized by a succulent compound fruit, thorny stems and oval, jagged-edged leaves. Blackberry is indigenous to the western United States, where it will often be found growing wild. The average bramble will grow to a height of three feet, and will spread rapidly

under good conditions. Like raspberries, blackberries are both a curse and a blessing in the garden. A well-established bramble will fruit throughout much of the summer, and the berries are welcome in the kitchen, where they make an excellent meat for jams and the perfect sweetener for cereals. But a hearty bramble, planted in rich, wet soil, will spread like the plague, and must be cut back several times each season. For this reason many gardeners consider the blackberry (and raspberry) bush to be a nuisance and will not plant it in their garden.

BLESSED THISTLE

Cnicus benedictus

Holy thistle, bitter thistle, spotted carduus

PERENNIAL

Blessed thistle has been used as a treatment for liver disorders, as well as menstrual problems. It is a very valuable herb. It seems to detoxify the liver. In many European countries blessed-thistle tablets are prescribed along with acetaminophen or aspirin to counterbalance the potential liver damage these drugs can cause. Many women take blessed thistle to regulate their periods. It seems to stimulate the appetite, and many herbalists prescribe it to their anorexic patients. Blessed thistle is found in any natural-food store in capsule form. It is often combined with other herbs that are beneficial to the liver, such as its close relative milk thistle, artichoke or red clover, to name a few. Blessed thistle is rarely, if ever, used as a garden plant.

BLOODROOT

Sanguinaria canadensis

Indian plant, tetterwort, red puccoon, sanguinaria, coonroot, redroot, sweet slumber

PERENNIAL

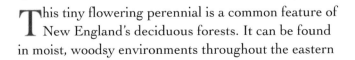

This tiny flowering perennial is a common feature of New England's deciduous forests. It can be found in moist, woodsy environments throughout the eastern United States.

Bloodroot's single-leafed, single-flowered stems sprout from a rhizome, which spreads at the base of large trees. The stem and roots are rich with a bright red-orange sap, which gives the plant its name. Native Americans used the sap as a potent dye, as well as a body paint. Bloodroot is a proven natural prophylactic against tooth decay and plaque buildup. Some commercial manufacturers even put small amounts of sanguinaria derivatives in their toothpaste. (This is not something to be experimented with in the home: sanguinaria is toxic.) Bloodroot is a hearty ornamental plant and will mix well with other flowering plants. Its simple, elegant flower makes a beautiful addition to the herb garden, or the casually cultivated flower garden.

BLUE COHOSH

Caulophyllum thalictroides

Papoose root, squaw root, blue ginseng, yellow ginseng

PERENNIAL

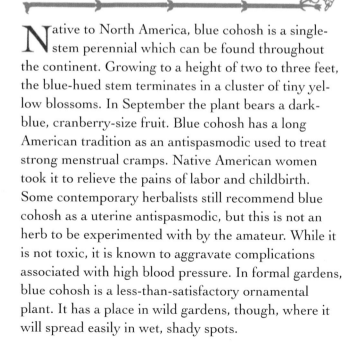

Native to North America, blue cohosh is a single-stem perennial which can be found throughout the continent. Growing to a height of two to three feet, the blue-hued stem terminates in a cluster of tiny yellow blossoms. In September the plant bears a dark-blue, cranberry-size fruit. Blue cohosh has a long American tradition as an antispasmodic used to treat strong menstrual cramps. Native American women took it to relieve the pains of labor and childbirth. Some contemporary herbalists still recommend blue cohosh as a uterine antispasmodic, but this is not an herb to be experimented with by the amateur. While it is not toxic, it is known to aggravate complications associated with high blood pressure. In formal gardens, blue cohosh is a less-than-satisfactory ornamental plant. It has a place in wild gardens, though, where it will spread easily in wet, shady spots.

BLUE FLAG

Iris versicolor, Iris pseudacorus

Iris, blue lily, liver lily, snake lily, poison lily, poison flag, flag lily, marsh iris, American fleur-de-lis

ANNUAL

Blue flag is the common name for the many species of wild blue iris that are native to North America. These exceptionally beautiful plants, with their blue-violet blossoms, grow wild in swampy, rich soil, in partial shade and full sun. They can be found throughout the western states, as far west as the Mississippi. Folk herbalists have traditionally ascribed dozens of medicinal applications to blue flag, but the amateur herbalist is strongly cautioned not to experiment with this plant. It is sometimes called "poison flag," and for good reason. The root and rhizome are actually toxic. Few sights are more beautiful than to come across a patch of wild blue flag in full bloom at the edge of a forest. The rich, almost luminescent blue of the early blossoms seems almost out of place against the greens and browns of the backdrop. It is blue flag's seductive blossom, and its ability to grow well in many different soils and light conditions, that has made it such a popular garden plant.

BONESET

Eupatorium perfoliatum

Feverwort, sweat plant, thoroughwort, Indian sage, ague weed, vegetable antimony

PERENNIAL

Boneset is a tall marsh weed that flowers in late August, spreading a large compound head of tiny white florets. It grows throughout North America in marshes and in soils rich with decaying foliage. It prefers full sun, but is an unusually hearty perennial and will grow almost anywhere. Boneset tea was used first by Native Americans, and later by European Americans, as a break-fever for especially bad colds and the flu. It was long thought that boneset could relieve the aches associated with fever and that it could bring down a high temperature. Modern researchers, however, have found no evidence to support such claims. Stripped of its medicinal properties, there is little to recommend boneset tea; it makes an unusually bitter brew. Although a field of boneset, blooming in the August sun, makes a beautiful summer scene, it is only marginally useful as an ornamental plant. Many regard it as an undesirable weed, though some will happily incorporate boneset into their wild gardens. Collect and dry the crowns in September. You'll find many uses for them in your herb crafting.

BORAGE

Borago officinalis

Starflower, beebread, burrage, false bugloss

     ANNUAL

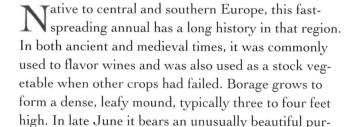

Native to central and southern Europe, this fast-spreading annual has a long history in that region. In both ancient and medieval times, it was commonly used to flavor wines and was also used as a stock vegetable when other crops had failed. Borage grows to form a dense, leafy mound, typically three to four feet high. In late June it bears an unusually beautiful purple-blue flower, with five petals, and black-tipped sta-

men. Both flowers and leaves are covered with whisker-like white hairs. Although contemporary herbalists find no medicinal uses for borage, it is still very much welcome in the kitchen. Its leaves will add a crisply subtle taste to stews and sauces, and the borage flower makes an excellent garnish on leafy salads. Because borage is a hearty, fast-growing plant, and because it is covered with such an attractive flower through midsummer, it is a popular addition to the backyard garden. Borage is easily sown from seed. Plant it in early spring, in medium-rich soil, and give it full sun.

BROOM

Sarothamnus scoparius, Cytisus scoparius

Scotch broom, broom tops, link, banal, hay weed

PERENNIAL

Broom, although used medicinally in the past, is too toxic to recommend as a healing herb today. It makes a lovely ornamental plant. Its lovely yellow flowers are some of the first to bloom in the spring. It is good for hedging and borders in the garden. It will grow well in sandy soils with lots of moisture in both the air and soil. Many of its parts are used in herbal crafting. The twigs can be made into baskets; the blooms can be dried and added to an herbal wreath.

BUCHU

Barosma betulina, barosma crenulata, barosma serratifolia

Bookoo, buku, bucku, bucco

PERENNIAL

Buchu, a native of Africa, is an effective "male" tonic. Taken regularly in capsule form or as an extract mixed with juice, it can help shrink enlarged prostate glands, alleviate the symptoms of urinary tract and prostate infections, and increase urination. If you have kidney problems, though, don't use it. It can irritate the kidneys. Consider another prostate herb, such as saw palmetto. Some women have reported that buchu also alleviates symptoms of premenstrual syndrome, most likely because of its diuretic properties.

Buchu was brought to the attention of European colonists in Africa, who brought the leaves back with them. It has been imported to North America for over 100 years, but it will only grow in Africa.

BUCKTHORN

Rhamnus cathartica, rhamnus frangula

Purging buckthorn, alder buckthorn, frangula, black dogwood, bird cherry, arrow wood

 PERENNIAL

This shrub grows to a height of six to eight feet. It has small ovate leaves and bears a tiny black seedberry in September and early November. Introduced to North America from Europe in the 18th century, it can be found throughout the Northeast, as far west as Ohio. The dried buckthorn berry has had a long history as an effective laxative. In Europe it has been used for centuries as a purgative and is well known among herbalists as a powerful, even violent, diuretic. Though some contemporary herbalists will still prescribe it, this is not a laxative to be experimented with in the home. Its action is too potent for most, and even moderate doses can induce vomiting and painful stomach cramps.

Aromatic Garden Herbs

If you decide to plant an herbal fragrance garden, the following herbs should be included, along with your personal favorites:

Lemon balm	**Rosemary**
Lemon thyme	**Scented geranium**
Nasturtiums	**Violet**

BURDOCK

Arctium lappa

Great burdock, burr, lappa, beggar's button, clothburr, hareburr, snake rhubarb, gobo, bardane, thorny burr

   BIENNIAL

Many species of burdock were introduced to this continent in past centuries. Several of these have made themselves common features of the landscape all over North America. Burdock is a tall weed with a rigid stalk, long leaves and clusters of tiny flowers, which bloom in July and then fall off, leaving behind a half-inch burr that is covered with tiny, sticky spikes. Burdock's sticky burrs are well-designed to catch a free ride by sticking to the coats of passing animals. Anyone who has ever walked through a tall-grass field in August, or through the roadside weeds, knows

Rejuvenating Miso Broth with Vegetables

1 cup burdock root, peeled and sliced
1 medium white onion, chopped fine
3 carrots, peeled and sliced
1 cup bok choy, peeled and sliced
2 stalks lemongrass, bruised slightly
2 tablespoons kelp powder
8 cups water
6 tablespoons cooked brown rice

Simmer all vegetables in water until tender. Remove lemongrass stalks. Dissolve the miso into the soup, and stir until well mixed. Taste and add more water if necessary. Add the rice. Lower heat and simmer for five more minutes. Serve piping hot. Serves six.

that the burdock burr sticks like Velcro to woolen and cotton clothing. Although most gardeners consider burdock to be a nuisance weed, this plant does have culinary value. It is an essential ingredient in many Asian dishes. In many regions of Europe and America, it is used as an inexpensive stock vegetable. The stalk, boiled or sautéed, adds its own mild flavor to soups and salads. The leaves can be sautéed like spinach and added to just about any kind of dish.

BUTCHER'S BROOM

Ruscus aculeatus

Sweet broom, box holly, Jew's myrtle

PERENNIAL

This member of the lily family is a popular treatment for leg cramps and arthritis. The plant contains steroidlike compounds that can reduce inflammation. It also is a mild diuretic and can help reduce swollen hemorrhoids. It is available in capsule and tincture form, as well as an ointment for hemorrhoids. It is also quite a lovely evergreen, which bears red berries in winter and is often used as Christmas decorations. It is also related to asparagus, and its very young, early shoots are edible and delicious when tossed into a spring salad. It is native to almost all of Europe and grows wild there, but it has been cultivated in North America. It will grow well even in poor soil, with little moisture.

CALENDULA
Calendula officinalis

Marigold, English marigold, pot marigold, mary bud

ANNUAL, BIENNIAL

This popular and familiar garden flower is one of the most useful herbs. It is a valuable medicinal; it is used in many commercial cosmetics; it is edible, and it is easy to grow. What more could you ask for in an herb? Much gentler than its cousin arnica, calendula makes a soothing salve for burns and other skin irritations, as well as relief for swelling. Calendula tea can be used as a mollifying wash for measles and chicken pox. It has been demonstrated to have some antibacterial qualities. Calendula tea may also be used internally to alleviate digestion problems and duodenal ulcers. It is useful in alleviating menstrual cramps and lowering fevers. In the kitchen calendula petals may be substituted for saffron. The petals and leaves may be tossed into salads, and the full flowers make beautiful edible decorations on cakes and pastries. Some dairies use the edible yellow dye produced by the petals to color butter. As a cosmetic, calendula is one of the most popular herbs used commercially in preparing hair dyes, creams, soaps and lotions. Although a European native, calendula will grow in just about any garden. It needs to be watered well and requires full sun or partial shade. The plant is quite hardy and will bloom through the winter in more temperate areas.

Hallucinations?

In the Middle Ages, calendula was added to many recipes. It was believed to enable people to see fairies.

CALIFORNIA POPPY
Eschscholzia californica

     ANNUAL

This bright orange wildflower is the state flower of California and can be seen blooming in abundance on hillsides and meadows throughout the spring and early summer. As a member of the poppy family, it has sedative qualities. Herbalists often use an extract in combination with other sedative herbs to make a sleeping aid. It is not illegal, like the opium poppy, and its sedative properties are mild in comparison. Nevertheless, it is a useful calming herb. Although it grows wild, it can be cultivated in a wildflower garden. It grows best in temperate climates where the mercury doesn't drop much below 50 degrees Fahrenheit. It is quite hardy and will flower in many soils, as long as it has full sun.

CAPER
Capparis spinosa
Caper bush

     PERENNIAL

The pickled unopened flower buds of the caper bush have been used as a condiment for centuries. They are native to the Mediterranean and north Africa. They have no known medicinal use. Capers are used in the kitchen to make sauces, garnish fish, create hors d'oeuvres, and make interesting vinaigrette dressings. The caper flowers are quite lovely. If you live in a warm climate, you may want to try growing this bush in your kitchen or ornamental garden. The white or pink flowers appear in early summer to late autumn, and they last only 24 hours.

CARAWAY

Carum carvi

Carum

BIENNIAL

Caraway is an ancient culinary herb that originated in the Middle East. It has been found fossilized at archaeological sites and has been mentioned in papyrus scrolls of ancient Egyptians. It is fair to say this herb has been in use for at least 5,000 years. It is a wild plant and grows well in most soils. It blooms with dozens of tiny white flowers and is quite fragrant. It is cultivated commercially, and in the garden, as a culinary herb. It has slight medicinal qualities. Chewing a few caraway seeds will help alleviate flatulence. It is a popular seasoning in a variety of cuisines. It is often used in seeded breads, especially rye. Its young leaves can be tossed into salads, and its root can be braised or boiled as a vegetable. It is also used to flavor various liqueurs such as kümmel.

Herbs in the Fossil Record

Caraway seed has been in use for at least 5,000 years. Remnants of these flavorful additions to rye bread have been found in Mesolithic food remnants.

CASCARA SAGRADA

Rhamnus purshiana

Cascara, chittem bark, California buckthorn, sacred bark

PERENNIAL

Cascara sagrada, a northern California native, was used for centuries as a laxative by Native Americans before the Spaniards arrived in the 16th century. They soon discovered this "wonder drug" was a mild laxative that worked. The 49ers during the gold rush found cascara to be a convenient herb, thus the name "chittem bark" derived from the more vulgar and descriptive "shittem bark." The popularity of cascara has endured. Many pharmaceutical companies use cascara in commercial laxatives. No synthetic chemical seems to be able to match the mildness and efficacy of the bark. You will find laxatives made with cascara in natural-food stores and pharmacies. Don't try to make your own laxative from the bark, though. The stripped bark must be aged for at least a year before it can be used. Fresh bark will cause nausea and terrible cramps. It is possible to grow the tree in other parts of North America for ornamental purposes. All you need is moist soil and full sun to partial shade. Keep in mind that the bark of these trees will have little medicinal value. Most cascara used medically today is still gathered from wild trees growing in California and the Pacific Northwest.

CASTOR BEAN

Ricinus communis

Palme christe, castor-oil plant, wonder tree

ANNUAL, PERENNIAL

As its name indicates, the castor-bean plant is the source of castor oil. It was used by ancient Egyptians as lamp oil and a base for ointments. It was, and is, considered an unsuitable culinary herb. Medicinally, it has been used internally as a regulating tonic for centuries. There may be something to this folk belief. Castor oil is high in protein and beneficial fatty acids, which can help lower cholesterol. It is available in most pharmacies.

CATNIP

Nepeta cataria

Catmint, catnep, field balm

PERENNIAL

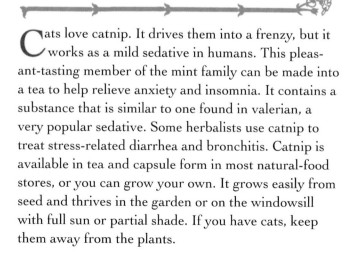

Cats love catnip. It drives them into a frenzy, but it works as a mild sedative in humans. This pleasant-tasting member of the mint family can be made into a tea to help relieve anxiety and insomnia. It contains a substance that is similar to one found in valerian, a very popular sedative. Some herbalists use catnip to treat stress-related diarrhea and bronchitis. Catnip is available in tea and capsule form in most natural-food stores, or you can grow your own. It grows easily from seed and thrives in the garden or on the windowsill with full sun or partial shade. If you have cats, keep them away from the plants.

> ### Calm Down
>
> Catnip may excite your kitty, but catnip tea is a mild and tasty sedative for humans. Try a cup before bedtime.

CAYENNE

Capsicum annuum, Capsicum frutescens

Redbird pepper, African pepper, chili, serrano, jalapeño, Anaheim hot, capsicum

     ANNUAL

Cayenne is a favorite herb in many cuisines. From Mexican to Indian to Thai to Creole and Cajun kitchens, and almost all points in between, cayenne can be found on spice racks or growing in many herb gardens. This fiery herb is a native of tropical America and didn't make its way to the Eastern Hemisphere until after Columbus's second voyage to the West Indies. It is now cultivated worldwide and has been hybridized into many different varieties—modulating from mild to extremely hot. It is the essential ingredient in Tabasco sauce and a must for a good salsa. Jamaican jerk sauce just wouldn't be the same without a good, hot habañero. Capsicum is also a good source of vitamin C, if you can stand the heat. It does have its place among the medicinal herbs. Most obvious is its ability to clear the sinuses. Taken in tea form, it is a mild stimulant. It encourages perspiration, the body's natural air-conditioning, which may partially explain why it is such a popular herb in hot climates. Eating cayenne or other hot spices temporarily increases the body's metabolic rate, and may cause one to burn calories more efficiently. It has been used topically in ointment form to treat shingles, but should never be applied to broken skin. Cayenne grows best in tropical climates, but it is possible to grow a pepper plant in your garden if you live in a relatively temperate area. Just give it lots of moisture and sunlight. Capsicum also makes a good houseplant—just be sure to warn your children not to eat the fruit!

CELANDINE

Chelidonium majus

Garden celandine, tetterwort, chelidonium, felonwort, Grecian may, wartweed, greater celanine

PERENNIAL

This attractive weed was once widely cultivated and used in herbal healing. It has fallen out of use, but is beginning to make a comeback as a medicinal herb. It can be dangerous, so never try to self-medicate with celandine. Make sure you consult with a trained herbalist. Its juice is used externally to clear up warts. It is used internally, with caution, to treat bladder inflammation and gallstones. In large doses it is a dangerous narcotic. It can be grown in your garden and will thrive in almost any soil under any conditions. Its yellow flowers make an attractive accent.

Temporary Toothache Relief

If you have a toothache, put a bruised clove or a drop of clove oil on the ailing tooth. This will soothe the pain until you get to the dentist.

CHAMOMILE

Chamaemelum nobile, Matricaria chamomilla,
Matricaria recutita

Roman chamomile, ground apple, German chamomile, wild
chamomile, mayweed

   PERENNIAL

Chamomile is one of the most popular and useful herbs used in the world today, and with good reason. Both *Chamaemelum* and *Matricaria* are wonderful additions to fragrant herb gardens. Roman chamomile

Ease Your Head

You can make a delicious tea that will also quiet a tension headache. Simply take one teaspoon of dried chamomile flowers, and steep them in one cup of boiling apple juice. Strain into a heated mug, and sip.

A Calming Bath

Add an infusion of chamomile flowers to an irritable child's (or adult's) bathwater for a soothing, calming soak.

(*Chamaemelum*) shares many medicinal properties with German chamomile (*Matricaria*), but it is bitter tasting and not as effective. The chamomile you'll find in stores and gardens will most likely be German chamomile. As a medicinal herb, it will treat a multitude of maladies. Chamomile tea is a pleasant bedtime treat. Its gentle sedative properties will help you sleep. But it is not soporific, so it is safe to drink during the day to relieve stress. Many women swear by chamomile when they get their periods. It alleviates cramps and back pain. It soothes indigestion and may actually prevent ulcers. Remember Peter Rabbit? Chamomile is one of the only herbs that is safe to give to children—it soothes colic and calms a hyperactive or distressed child. Its has antibacterial qualities. A chamomile poultice can reduce and soothe swollen joints and muscles. Many commercial cosmetics contain chamomile. It is used in facial creams, shampoos, dry skin and acne treatments. To relieve eyestrain, take two chamomile tea bags, and steep them in hot water for a few minutes, let them cool a bit, then place them on your eyes. It is a heavenly respite! The daisylike flowers of the German chamomile look lovely in any garden. They are best started from seed in sandy soil, and thrive in full sun. They do not need much water.

When the plants start to flower, you can harvest them and make your own herbal preparations. Chamomile is a cash crop in many countries.

CHAPARRAL

Larrea tridenta

Creosote bush, greasewood, stinkweed

 PERENNIAL

C haparral is a controversial herb, because it is a powerful antioxidant. Many herbalists believe it reduces cancerous tumors and use it as a treatment for melanoma. This has not been clinically proven. The evidence, and there is much of it, is largely anecdotal. If you are diagnosed with cancer, do not use chaparral without consulting your doctor.

Chaparral tastes awful, but it is useful in treating gum disease and tooth decay, since it is an antiseptic and natural antibiotic. Chaparral grows wild in the American Southwest, and is not suitable for gardens. You may have difficulty finding it, even in a well-stocked natural-food store, because of the controversy surrounding it.

CHERRY

Prunus virginiana, Prunus serotina

Wild black cherry, chokecherry, wild cherry bark, Virginia prune bark, whiskey cherry, rum cherry, black cherry

   PERENNIAL

It's no accident that many cough remedies come cherry flavored. Wild cherry bark is a soothing tonic for sore throats and coughs. It is also used to treat bronchitis. If you decide to prepare your own cherry-bark tea, do not boil the bark. It diminishes the soothing properties. Simply soak the bark in hot water for several hours. This bark infusion will work nicely. Cherries are used in cooking and baking and are delicious eaten out of hand. Wild cherries are slightly bitter, but can also be eaten. They are best in jams and preserves and make an interesting addition to chutney. Their extract is used to flavor certain liqueurs. *Prunus virginiana* is a beautiful tree, offering fragrant blossoms in the spring and fruit in the late summer. It grows best in the mid-Atlantic states.

CHERVIL

Anthriscus cerefolium

Pleuches de cerfeuille, garden chervil

ANNUAL

Chervil is a popular culinary herb, especially in France. It complements most savory dishes and is an ingredient in *herbes de Provence*. It is an annual, sweet-smelling herb that will grow well in a window garden or kitchen garden. If it is kept in a sunny spot indoors in the winter, it will give you fresh chervil to cook with all year round. Its flowers, which appear in the summer, can be used in salads and as garnish. As a medicinal herb, it is used in teas to treat indigestion and as a general tonic to stimulate the metabolism. A warm chervil poultice will soothe achy joints.

CHICORY

Cichorium intybus

Succory, blue sailors, blue dandelion, wild endive, leaf chicory

PERENNIAL

Chicory is best known as a coffee substitute and a salad green. It is a nutritious culinary herb, loaded with vitamins B, C, K and P, as well as many beneficial minerals. Its leaves have a slightly bitter, but

CHICORY

not unpleasant, taste, and it mixes well with other field greens in a salad. The dried root can be ground and used as a coffee substitute or to augment coffee. Coffee with chicory is quite popular in New Orleans. Chicory is as easy to grow as any green. It should be planted in well-fertilized soil. It will provide fresh greens throughout the summer months.

Sprout Prevention

To keep your potatoes from sprouting in the vegetable drawer or root cellar, store them with sprigs of thyme, peppermint and cinnamon bark.

CHIVE

Allium schoenoprasum

Allium

   PERENNIAL

A llium is part of the onion family, and it is the only member that grows wild in North America. It can be used like garlic in the kitchen, but it must be used in larger quantities to achieve the same bite. It is also chopped and served as a garnish for vegetables, tossed into salads, and used to season soups. It grows easily in a kitchen garden or on a windowsill. It must be used fresh. Dried chives lose their flavor.

CINNAMON

Cinnamomum zeylanicum, Cinnamomum verum

Cinnamon tree, Ceylon cinnamon

    PERENNIAL

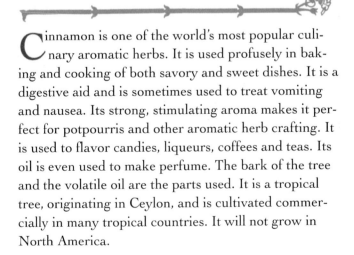

C innamon is one of the world's most popular culinary aromatic herbs. It is used profusely in baking and cooking of both savory and sweet dishes. It is a digestive aid and is sometimes used to treat vomiting and nausea. Its strong, stimulating aroma makes it perfect for potpourris and other aromatic herb crafting. It is used to flavor candies, liqueurs, coffees and teas. Its oil is even used to make perfume. The bark of the tree and the volatile oil are the parts used. It is a tropical tree, originating in Ceylon, and is cultivated commercially in many tropical countries. It will not grow in North America.

CLARY

Salvia sclarea

Muscatel sage, clary sage

BIENNIAL

Clary, a variety of sage, is widely cultivated for its oil which is used in making perfume. It is a pleasant-smelling, attractive garden herb and blooms with numerous pink, white, and light purple flowers. It is occasionally used as a medicinal herb to soothe irritable stomachs, but its main uses are decorative and cosmetic.

CLEAVERS
Galium aparine

Bedstraw, catchstraw, goosegrass, clivers, cleaverwort

 ANNUAL

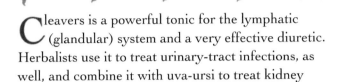

Cleavers is a powerful tonic for the lymphatic (glandular) system and a very effective diuretic. Herbalists use it to treat urinary-tract infections, as well, and combine it with uva-ursi to treat kidney

stones. A poultice or ointment made from cleavers is used externally to treat many skin ailments. It is a weed native to Europe, but grows wild throughout North America as well. It is rarely, if ever, used as a garden herb.

CLOVE

Syzygium aromaticum, Caryophyllus aromaticus

Clavos, caryophyllus, clove tree

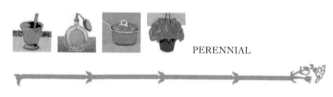

PERENNIAL

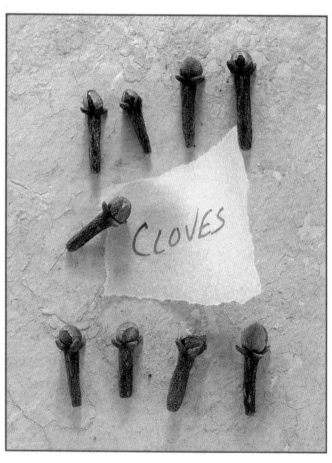

Clove is one of the most aromatic of the healing herbs and has many uses in the kitchen as well. It is an Asian evergreen and does not grow in North America. Dentists use clove oil as a topical anesthetic. It will also temporarily relieve a toothache until proper treatment can be obtained. It is a common ingredient in many commercial mouthwashes and toothpastes. Taken as a tea, it is a digestive aid. In the kitchen cloves are essential when making mulled wine or cider. Ground cloves are used in curries and sauces and add an interesting flavor to stews.

COFFEE

Coffea arabica

Java, joe

PERENNIAL

There is nothing like a good cup of coffee. When those roasted brown berries yield their elixir to boiled water, a simple pleasure is born. People have been growing coffee in Mexico and South America for centuries. Early European colonists discovered this ancient brew in South America and Africa and brought it back home with them, and the culture of the coffeehouse was born. But coffee was not only used as a pleasurable drink. It was also considered a medicinal herb because of its stimulant qualities. To this day, caffeine is the preferred legal chemical stimulus. Caffeine, especially in the form of strong black coffee, can help stave off migraine headaches. Many migraine sufferers will drink a hot cup of coffee just as they feel the migraine "aura" descending on them. Many perspiration migraine medications contain caffeine as well. Coffee flavors everything from barbecue sauce to ice cream. It is used in many sweet and savory dishes.

Coffee drinks have become a staple of any decent menu. There's probably a café on your corner where you can pick up your daily mocha or double latte. If you want to grow your own coffee, it will be difficult, unless, of course, you live in South America. Coffee plants take up to five years to fruit, and the best beans are grown at an altitude of 4,500 feet or higher. But coffee plants make attractive houseplants. Give them lots of sunshine and water, and you will have an unusual and attractive ornamental.

COLTSFOOT

Tussilago farfara

Coughwort, bull's foot, horsehoof, foal's foot, Tussilago

PERENNIAL

Coltsfoot grows wild throughout Europe and North America. Its large yellow, marigoldlike flowers have a pleasant aroma and bloom before its leaves appear. Coltsfoot makes a fascinating addition to an aromatic herb garden. It grows best in moist soil, with partial shade. Like chaparral, it is a controversial herb. Although it is an excellent remedy for respiratory ailments, it contains certain alkaloids that can cause liver damage with prolonged use. If you have had any liver-related diseases, do not use this herb. Those with healthy livers may want to look for a less problematic herb to treat their bronchial problems.

COMFREY

Symphytum officinale

Gum plant, healing herb, knit bone, nip bone, bruisewort, knitback, assear, consoloda

PERENNIAL

Comfrey has a long history. The Greeks made a paste of it to treat wounds and broken bones externally and drank comfrey tea for respiratory and digestive problems. Centuries later, herbalists were still using it to treat bronchitis and diarrhea. Comfrey is another controversial herb, though. It contains chemicals that have been shown to be carcinogenic in labora-

SOAPWORT

tory animals. But it also contains allantoin, a chemical
that promotes new cell growth, as well as tumor-fight-
ing agents. This may negate its cancer-causing aspects.
Comfrey can cause liver damage, but it also contains a
good amount of antioxidants. There has yet to be any
consensus on comfrey. Herbalists contend that the
chances of comfrey causing cancer are about the same
as the risk of eating one peanut-butter sandwich.
Conservative scientists discourage its use completely.
Comfrey tea is a safe digestive aid, but it should never
be ingested in any form other than a weak tea. There
are better herbs to treat indigestion. In the garden
comfrey is a friend. It is a hardy plant that can grow to
be as tall as six feet. It has striking bell-shaped flowers,

which may be white, purple or blue. It grows in well-drained soil with full sun or partial shade.

CORIANDER

Coriandrum sativum

Cilantro, Chinese parsley

ANNUAL

Coriander is a popular culinary herb, especially in Asian and Mexican cuisines. The ground seeds are used in curries, and the fresh leaves, known as cilantro, are used in many South American recipes. The whole seeds are used in baking. The roots may be cooked and eaten as a vegetable, but it is an acquired taste. Coriander also flavors many liqueurs and can-

---

Sesame Cilantro Pesto Sauce

3 cloves garlic, peeled
2 teaspoons peeled, chopped ginger
⅓ cup toasted sesame seeds
2 bunches fresh cilantro, leaves only
1 tablespoon mirin or rice wine
1 tablespoon soy sauce
2 tablespoons fresh lime juice
¼ teaspoon red-hot sauce, or to taste
⅓ cup sesame oil

Combine garlic and ginger in a food processor or blender. Add sesame seeds and cilantro leaves and blend until mixture is finely chopped. Turn off food processor. Add mirin, soy sauce, lime juice and hot sauce. Turn on food processor, and slowly add sesame oil until pesto is smooth and creamy. Serve over buckwheat pasta. Do not heat pesto. Serves four.

dies. Medicinally, the bruised seed is made into a poultice to relieve joint pain. Chewing the seeds aids digestion. Coriander is easy to grow from seed. It prefers dry soil and full sun.

Herbal Bookmark

Since the first colonists landed in North America, costmary leaves have been used as bookmarks in Bibles and prayer books. It not only saved the place, but its minty aroma kept the churchgoer awake.

COSTMARY

Chrysanthemum balsamita

Bible leaf, alecost, balsam herb

PERENNIAL

This pleasant-smelling aromatic herb has been used for centuries in making perfume. It was used in ointments to soothe burns, but is rarely treated as a medicinal herb today. Its uses as a culinary herb are manifold. Its dried leaves and flowers are used to flavor homemade beer and wine, soups, cakes and

poultry. It is a nice addition to a potpourri, and is used as a stimulating scent in aromatherapy. It makes an attractive garden plant. It will grow in most soils and light conditions, but it will not flower if it is grown in the shade.

CRAMP BARK
Viburnum opulus

High cranberry, guelder rose, squaw bush, snowball tree, European cranberry, viburnum

PERENNIAL

Cramp bark, or the guelder rose, is an attractive ornamental herb. It can grow as high as ten feet, and shows off lovely white flowers and purple fruit. It is native to Europe, northern Asia and North Africa, but has been introduced into gardens worldwide. It needs moist soil, and will flourish in full sun or partial shade. The raw berries are poisonous, but can be cooked and eaten like cranberries. The cooked berries are also distilled into a liquor in some Scandinavian countries. Medicinally, the name says it all. Viburnum is very effective in relieving menstrual cramps and is a uterine sedative. It also helps relieve premenstrual syndrome and is even used to relieve cramps during pregnancy. (NOTE: Do not use cramp bark while pregnant unless you have your doctor's approval.) It is usually taken as a tea and often combined with other soothing herbs. It is readily available in natural-food stores in tea or capsule form.

CRANESBILL

Geranium maculatum

Alumroot, wild geranium, wild cranesbill, storksbill, dove's foot, chocolate flower, spotted cranesbill, American cranesbill

 PERENNIAL

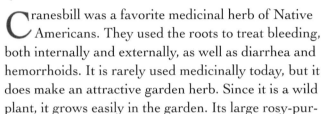

Cranesbill was a favorite medicinal herb of Native Americans. They used the roots to treat bleeding, both internally and externally, as well as diarrhea and hemorrhoids. It is rarely used medicinally today, but it does make an attractive garden herb. Since it is a wild plant, it grows easily in the garden. Its large rosy-purple flowers are quite striking.

CROCUS SAFFRON

Crocus sativa

Saffron, Spanish saffron

 PERENNIAL

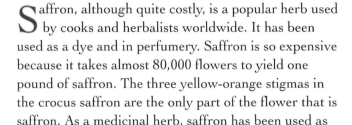

Saffron, although quite costly, is a popular herb used by cooks and herbalists worldwide. It has been used as a dye and in perfumery. Saffron is so expensive because it takes almost 80,000 flowers to yield one pound of saffron. The three yellow-orange stigmas in the crocus saffron are the only part of the flower that is saffron. As a medicinal herb, saffron has been used as everything from a pulmonary tonic to an antidepressant, but modern herbalists concur that its uses are not all encompassing. It is used today primarily as a sedative, pain reliever and digestive aid. It is also recommended to promote menstruation. Most recently it has been the subject of animal research, which has yielded some interesting results. It seems that saffron may indeed reduce cholesterol, help clear artery-clogging deposits, and lower blood pressure. Taken as a daily tea, it may be quite beneficial. In the kitchen it is a prized and precious herb. A little goes a long way. It is used to flavor *paella* and other Spanish dishes. It enhances shellfish and rice. You can grow crocus saffron in your garden, but the best saffron is imported.

CUMIN
Cuminum cyminum

     ANNUAL

Cumin seeds have been used in cooking for thousands of years. Romans ground it and used it like black pepper. It is used mainly today in curries and other Indian dishes. The seeds are also used in pickling, and the oil is used in perfumery. Cumin seeds are often served after an Indian meal to be chewed as a digestive aid. Although this plant is thought of as a warm-climate herb, it will grow almost anywhere, as long as it is planted in a sunny spot in well-drained soil. It blooms with small white or pink flowers and is sweet smelling.

Herbal Aphrodisiacs
Damiana leaf, kelp, cayenne, artichokes, asparagus and garlic are all said to be aphrodisiacs for men and women. Ginseng is thought to be a male aphrodisiac, and dong quai, a woman's.

DAMIANA

Turnera diffusa, Turnera aphrodisiaca

Mexican damiana, pastorata, hierba del venado

PERENNIAL

Damiana has a reputation as a "male" aphrodisiac, and although most of the claims cannot be clinically substantiated, anecdotal evidence indicates that there may be something to the assertion. It is a far safer herb than yohimbe, so if you're looking for a "male" aphrodisiac, you may want to try some damiana. It is usually available in extract form at most natural-food stores or as a tea. It is a stimulant, so you should start with a small dosage, and see how it affects you. It may cause nausea, so it is recommended that it be combined with nux vomica. Damiana is a native of South America and the most southwestern parts of the United States. It is a small shrub and has yellow flowers. If you live in these areas, you can easily grow it in your garden. It grows best in dry soil with full sun, and may bloom year-round.

DANDELION

Taraxacum officinale

Lion's tooth, fairy clock, pissenlit, thick-leafed dandelion, blowballs, doonheadclock, yellow gowan, priest's crown

PERENNIAL

This garden weed is actually one of our most useful herbs. As a medicinal herb, it is a good diuretic and may relieve the bloating of premenstrual syndrome. Dandelion-root tea is a good liver tonic and a

DANDELION

Beneficial Weed

If dandelion appears in your fruit orchard or vegetable patch, think twice before you remove it. Dandelion attracts bees and other pollinating insects, as well as emitting a gas that encourages ripening.

digestive aid. The entire plant is edible and loaded with vitamins A and C. In the spring, young fresh dandelion leaves make a tasty and nutritious addition to salads. The leaves may be cooked like any other leafy vegetable. Older leaves will be bitter, so be sure only to choose young ones. Dried and powdered dandelion root may be used as a coffee substitute. Many people make homemade dandelion wine in the spring. Check your family cookbook for a recipe.

DEVIL'S CLAW

Harpagophytum procumbrens

Grapple plant, devil's craw root

PERENNIAL

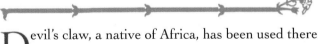

D evil's claw, a native of Africa, has been used there for centuries as a remedy for arthritis and other inflammations. It has certain properties that mimic cortisone. It has become a popular herbal treatment in Europe and is gaining popularity in North America. It's also used to treat gout. The roots of the plant are used in treatment, and you should be able to find capsules or tinctures at your natural-food store. Since devil's claw is a native of Africa, it is rarely grown here. If you are pregnant or nursing, do not use devil's claw.

DILL

Anethum graveolens

Dill weed, dill seed

ANNUAL

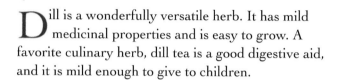

Dill is a wonderfully versatile herb. It has mild medicinal properties and is easy to grow. A favorite culinary herb, dill tea is a good digestive aid, and it is mild enough to give to children.

Spicy Garlic Dill Pickles:

4 lbs. kirby cucumbers
2 cups of white vinegar
2 to 3 cups water
4 tablespoons kosher salt
10 garlic cloves, peeled
2 jalapeño peppers, seeded and sliced
4 teaspoons dill seed
4 sprigs fresh dill
4 sprigs fresh tarragon
3 bay leaves
1 teaspoon whole black peppercorns

Combine all ingredients in a large stockpot or soup kettle. Bring to a boil. Add more water if necessary. Turn off heat, and cool. Pour entire contents of pot into a large glass jar or stoneware crock. Cover loosely with waxed paper or plastic wrap. Let stand in refrigerator for at least two weeks before use.

DOCK

Rumex Crispus

Yellow dock, curled dock, rumex

PERENNIAL

Closely related to sorrel, dock is native to central Europe and has been widely naturalized to temperate areas throughout the world. In North America it is a common sight, generally regarded as a roadside weed. Dock's large, tapering taproot issues a thick stem, which typically grows to a height of three feet. Its hundreds of tiny yellow flowers are densely clustered along the stem and along short branches. Its spear-shaped leaves are largest at the bottom, where they can grow to ten inches long. From a distance, dock is easily mistaken for goldenrod. While its close cousin sorrel has a distinguished culinary past, dock's primary uses throughout history have been medicinal. The ancients used dock as an effective laxative, and it is still used for that purpose by European and American herbalists alike. Although the serious herbalist is likely to have dried dock root on hand, she will not have gotten it from her garden. Dock is a prolific weed, and is difficult to control once it is established. Because it is so easily gathered in the wild, it is not recommended as a garden herb, unless planted in a contained and isolated area.

DONG QUAI

Angelica sinensis, Angelica polymorpha

 PERENNIAL

D ong Quai is a useful "female" tonic. Taken in tea or capsule form, it helps relieve menstrual cramps and may increase fertility. Since it is a uterine relaxant, never use it if you are pregnant. It is also a stimulant even more powerful than caffeine. It is available in capsule form at most natural-food stores.

ECHINACEA

Echinacea angustifolia, Echinacea purpurea, Echinacea pallida

Purple coneflower, black sampson, rudbeckia, Missouri coneflower

 PERENNIAL

This beautiful wildflower is native to North
America, where it grows in dry prairie lands from
the Gulf states into Canada. It is easily recognized by
its singularly beautiful flower, with delicate pastel-
purple petals radiating from the prominent red-orange
corona, which looks something like a pincushion. From
its base echinacea issues large lobed leaves on long
stems. Blooming in late July through August, there
are few sights so extraordinary as a meadow filled
with echinacea after good rains in May and June.
Echinacea has had an important history as a medicinal
herb. Native Americans understood its effectiveness as
an antibiotic and introduced it to the Europeans as a
poultice that would quicken the healing of all sorts of

wounds. Before the development of antibiotics, echinacea had widespread commercial use in the United States as an important ingredient in healing ointments. The best reason to include echinacea in your flower garden is its beautiful pastel flower. Still able to bloom in September, it will bring color to your garden when other plants are past flowering. Echinacea is a low-maintenance plant, easily sown from seed. Plant it in full sun, and give it well-drained, well-composted soil.

EPAZOTE

Chenopodium ambrosioides, Chenopodium anthelminticum

Mexican tea, wormseed, Jerusalem tea, Spanish tea, ambrosia, stickweed, goosefoot, stinking weed

  ANNUAL, PERENNIAL

This Mexican native has spread all over North America, but it is little known as more than a weed north of the border. However, it is an essential part of Mexican cuisine. Small amounts are essential to proper preparation of refried beans and other bean-based dishes. Epazote not only lends a pungent flavor to these dishes, it helps alleviate flatulence. It is employed as a tea to stimulate milk flow in lactating mothers and supposedly helps relieve postpartum pain. Large doses are poisonous, but as a light tea or a pinch in a bean recipe, epazote is perfectly safe. It is an unattractive plant, and it doesn't smell very good, but you may want to consider growing it in a kitchen garden, especially if you are interested in Mexican cooking.

EPHEDRA

Ephedra sinica, Ephedra equistina, Ephedra intermedia

Ma Huang

 PERENNIAL

Ephedra has been gaining a well-deserved reputation as an antihistamine. Taken in capsule form or in a tea, it can alleviate congestion from colds and allergies. The commercial over-the-counter drug Sudafed is derived from this plant. It is also a powerful stimulant. If you are using it to treat a cold or allergy, do not use it at night, for it will keep you awake.

EUCALYPTUS

Eucalyptus globulus, Eucalyptus citridora, Eucalyptus compacta

Blue Gum eucalyptus, lemon-scented gum

 PERENNIAL

There are over 300 species of eucalyptus, all indigenous to Australia and the surrounding islands. It was brought to California years ago, where it has thrived. It is a very drought-resistant plant and has no natural antagonists in California, so its growth has been unchecked for decades. It has overrun many native plants, and some consider it a great nuisance. However, it is a lovely tree with a wonderful, intoxicating aroma. Its oil is used as an antiseptic and deodorant. It is a natural insect repellent. Its vapor is inhaled to clear congested chests. It is rarely used internally. It can be added to simmering potpourris, and its dried branches and leaves can be used in aromatic herb crafting.

Breathe Free

To relieve bronchitis or blocked sinuses, add three to five drops of eucalyptus oil to your vaporizer.

EVENING PRIMROSE

Oenothera biennis

Cabish, cure-all, tree primrose, tall sundrop, evening star

ANNUAL, BIENNIAL

This American native is a valuable medicinal herb and a lovely garden plant. Recent studies have shown that its oil is high in unsaturated fatty acids, which may prevent heart attacks. Doctors are begin-

91

ning to recommend it to their heart patients as a prophylactic. It is also useful in alleviating symptoms of
premenstrual syndrome. All parts of the plant are edible. The flowers can be used in salads or as garnish.
The roots can be boiled and served as a vegetable. It is
a very interesting garden plant. Evening star, one of its
common names, refers to the fact that the yellow petals
emit an eerie phosphorescent light in the evening. It
will grow well in most soils, as long as it has full sun.

EYEBRIGHT
Euphrasia officinalis

Meadow eyebright

 PERENNIAL

This medicinal herb is used primarily to treat eye problems. In ointment or drops it is an effective treatment for conjunctivitis. It is also sometimes used as a nasal spray to soothe irritated sinuses. It can be used as a poultice to help wounds heal faster. It is available at most natural-food stores.

FALSE INDIGO
Baptisia tinctoria

Wild indigo, indigo broom, horsefly weed, dyer's bartista

  PERENNIAL

This native herb can be found growing in wooded areas in the northeastern states, as far south as the Carolinas. It can be recognized by its fruit, which forms a pealike pod. False indigo has a branching stem, each shoot terminating in a cluster of three simple ovate leaflets. The yellow flower appears in May and June. Traditionally, the chief use for this plant is as dyestuff, but it has had medicinal uses as well. Western herbalists recommend it for low-grade fevers, while some Native American tribes believe that it is useful for treating cancer. False indigo is easy to sow from seed and easy to maintain. Its flowers alone earn it a place in the herb garden, but the plant becomes brownish and weedy by late July and August. Dry the seedpods in a cool room to use for craft projects.

FENNEL

Foeniculum vulgare, Foeniculum dulce

Florence fennel, finnochio

PERENNIAL

Fennel is native to Mediterranean regions, but has been naturalized to temperate areas around the world, including parts of California. Closely related to dill, fennel has many of the same features. Its straight stem branches toward the top and terminates in radial shoots that support the yellow florets. Leaf clusters grow from axles at distant intervals along the stem. Like dill, the leaves form fine branching needles. Although fennel tea has a long history in the West as an excellent remedy for an upset stomach, it is most valued as a culinary herb. Southern Italian cuisine calls for fennel in many recipes. Use the delicate leaves as a garnish in salads. Its subtle sweetness makes it a perfect flavoring for baked whitefish. Bake fennel into your wheat breads to add a delicate sweetness. If you live in an area where the winters are harsh, you must do a little work to cultivate fennel. Unearth the bulbs in early November, and winter them in a bucket of dry soil, in a cool and arid location.

Sweeten Your Breath

To cure bad breath, chew on some fennel seeds.

Sweet and Crunchy Snack

Sliced fennel bulb is a crunchy and tasty addition to any crudités platter.

FENUGREEK
Trigonella foenumgraecum

Hu Lu Ba

     ANNUAL

Native to Indochina, as well as the Mediterranean, fenugreek has been naturalized to many other regions in the world and is commonly used as commercial fodder for livestock. This is a small, succulent, fast-growing annual, characterized by tripartite, dentate leaves. Fennel flowers in July and bears pealike seedpods, two to three inches in length.

Fenugreek tea, made from the dried seeds, is used by diverse cultures as a laxative and as a remedy for ulcers. It is valued also as a culinary herb, especially in those regions where it is native. Northern African cuisine relies heavily on fenugreek for the unique flavor it lends to meats and poultry.

In temperate regions, fenugreek can easily be sown in the vegetable garden. It require a rich, moist soil and plenty of full sun.

FEVERFEW

Chrysanthemum parthenium, Tanacetum parthenium

   PERENNIAL

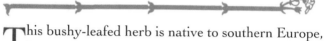

This bushy-leafed herb is native to southern Europe, but has been introduced to many other parts of the world, including North America. Feverfew's leaves are complex and highly dentate. Flowers are daisylike,

with tiny, delicate petals. Feverfew is especially valuable as a medicinal, and has become a popular remedy for migraine headaches and for menstrual headaches. It has been demonstrated to be effective not only for relieving severe headaches, but for treating arthritis as well. Those who suffer from chronic migraine headaches will likely benefit from a small daily dose of feverfew. Leaves should be eaten fresh and raw, no more than three a day. Because the leaves are bitter, those people who rely on them as a medicinal will often mix them with other foods to mask their unpleasant taste. Feverfew is worth planting for its ornate features alone. In midsummer a single plant will bear as many as 25 delicate yellow-and-white flowers.

FIG

Ficus carica

Common fig

PERENNIAL

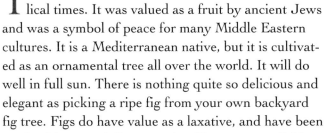

The common fig has been with civilization since biblical times. It was valued as a fruit by ancient Jews and was a symbol of peace for many Middle Eastern cultures. It is a Mediterranean native, but it is cultivated as an ornamental tree all over the world. It will do well in full sun. There is nothing quite so delicious and elegant as picking a ripe fig from your own backyard fig tree. Figs do have value as a laxative, and have been used safely as such for centuries. Fig syrup, available in some natural-food stores, is a laxative treatment, but it is possible to make your own. Figs are used widely in cooking—from pastries and cookies to jams and jellies. Dried figs are often a component of fruitcakes.

FLAX

Linum usitatissimum

Flaxseed, linseed

PERENNIAL

Although this plant is native to southern Europe and northern Africa, it has been so vitally important to so many cultures over the centuries that it has been introduced to virtually every corner of the globe. Flax is a single-stem plant that grows upward and straight, branching at the top, and terminating with blue five-petaled flowers. Bladed leaves alternate at regular intervals along the stem and branches. Since ancient times flax has been an indispensable crop, providing the raw material for the linen used in clothing, canvases and nets. Since the Flemish invention of oil-based paints in the 14th century, flax has been commercially important as a source of linseed oil. Although flax has some useful medicinal properties, the amateur herbalist should not experiment with it, since some parts of the plant are toxic. However, recent studies of flaxseed and flax oil have shown that these products of the plant may be useful in reducing "bad" cholesterol. Many natural-food stores now sell flax oil as an herbal treatment and flax seeds to be baked into breads. However, flax makes a very satisfying ornamental plant, with its blue flowers hanging high above the bushier herbs in the garden. It is easy to sow from seed and can be treated either as a perennial or as an annual.

Garden Fresh

For maximum flavor, add fresh herbs to any slow-cooking stew or soup during the last 20 minutes of cooking.

FLEABANE

Erigeron canadensis

Canadian fleabane, horseweed, hog weed, butterweed, colt's tail, pride weed

PERENNIAL

Fleabane is the most common member of the Erigeron family and is related to the daisy. It is identified by its stiff, straight stem, which branches toward the top and terminates in conical, somewhat thistlelike white flowers. Fleabane is native to North America, where it is most often considered to be a nuisance weed. It is a prolific self-sower and will find a place for itself just about anywhere the soil is rich and wet. Although fleabane was highly valued by the colonists as a medicinal, the contemporary herbalist finds only limited uses for it, primarily as an astringent. Fleabane is useful for treating a sore throat, but the leaves are so bitter that any decoctions must be heavily laced with sugar or honey. Fleabane's decidedly weedlike appearance does not recommend it as an ornamental.

FOXGLOVE

Digitalis purpurea

Fairy thimbles, thimbles, folk's glove

BIENNIAL

Foxglove is native to southern Europe and northern Africa, but is cultivated as an ornate plant throughout many of the world's temperate regions. This is a single-stem plant, with soft, broad leaves at the base, and a stunning cluster of coronet-shaped flowers issuing radially, up the top half of the long stem. Foxglove's blossom, which shows itself midsummer, ranges in color from white to a deep crimson blush. As a medicinal, foxglove provides an essential ingredient for certain cardiopulmonary irregularities. But it must never be ingested except under strict medical supervision; foxglove is one of the most poisonous of herbs. While it has no medicinal or culinary applications in the home, foxglove is highly prized by the flower gardener. It puts on an extraordinary show in June and July, each plant bearing dozens of graceful, colorful blossoms. If you have children, you must resist the temptation to include foxglove in your garden—even moderate doses from the leaf or flower can be fatal to a child.

FRENCH MARIGOLD
Tagetes patula

ANNUAL

French marigolds are perfect garden flowers. They are easy to grow from seed and will flourish in full sun in many climates. They are originally from Mexico, where early Aztecs fed the petals to their chickens to color the shells of the eggs. Tagetes became quite popular in European gardens and remains a favorite for many gardeners worldwide. Not only are French marigolds pretty, they act as natural insect repellents. They repel white flies, a common garden pest, and actually seem to attack some other insects. The Aztecs used marigold flowers to treat dysentery and coughs, and Chinese herbalists still use tagetes to treat whooping cough. But French marigolds are best in gardens. A tea of the dried petals will kill mosquito larvae. French—marigold oil is used as a flavoring in many commercial food products, such as ice cream, puddings, condiments and some alcoholic beverages.

FRINGE TREE
Chionanthus virginicus

Poison ash, snowdrop tree, old man's beard, white fringe, flowering ash, graybeard tree, shavings, snowflowers

PERENNIAL

The fringe tree's name derives from when it is in bloom. It then appears to have grown beautiful white fringes, or is covered with snow. A North American native, it is cultivated widely as an ornamental tree, but it does have limited medicinal value. The bark and dried roots have been used in poultices for skin inflammations. A tonic made from the fringe tree was often used as a liver stimulant, but this practice is no longer popular. There are more effective liver tonics.

Tummy Tonics

A tea made from any of these herbs, fresh or dried, or a combination of two or more of them, is a wonderful digestive aid:

Anise seed	Licorice
Basil	Peppermint
Caraway seeds	Raspberry
Chamomile	Yarrow
Ginger	

GARLIC

Allium sativum

Stinking rose, clove garlic

PERENNIAL

Garlic is a member of the onion family, with its characteristic compound bulb lined with a delicate husk. It issues its long, bladed leaves from a single stalk, which terminates with a floral umbel, bearing a cluster of tiny, almost inconspicuous florets. Probably indigenous to the Baltic region, garlic was long ago introduced to other continents and has become an essential culinary tool to almost every culture in the world. Garlic's culinary worth need hardly be extolled, since it is so highly prized among even the most amateur chefs. In southern French and Italian cuisine it is simply essential. Garlic has a long history as a medicinal as well. While modern science does not substantiate garlic's power to ward off evil spirits, there is good evidence that garlic helps to lower cholesterol levels and

Cough and Cold Comfort

Garlic and honey make a wonderfully soothing cough and sore-throat syrup. You will need four ounces of honey, four ounces of peeled, chopped garlic cloves, and four ounces of water. Warm the honey and water over low heat until it has liquefied. Stir gently. Place the garlic cloves in a glass jar. Pour the liquefied honey-and-water mixture over the garlic. Stir the mixture, and let it cool. Place the lid loosely on the jar and let sit for about two weeks. It will then be ready for use to heal sore throats. Take one teaspoon as needed.

bring down high blood pressure. One reason for the generally excellent cardiopulmonary health among Italian men, may be the amount of garlic they consume. If you would like the garlic in your kitchen to come from your own backyard, try planting a few cloves in early spring. Garlic is a hearty plant and will do well in dry soil, so long as it is richly composted. Pull the bulbs in mid- to late summer when the leaves have fallen back. Garlic's floral umber has rather an exotic form. It dries well when hung upside down and makes a good addition to the dried herbal bouquet.

GENTIAN
Gentiana lutea

Yellow gentian, bitterroot

PERENNIAL

Gentian is a flowering herb characterized by a tall, very straight stem, with clusters of leaves and flowers together at regular intervals along the stalk. The flowers are clustered, long blooming and usually yellowish-brown in color. Tonics made from gentian root have been used for centuries as a digestive aid, and its effectiveness in this capacity is supported by contemporary research. Be warned that gentian root makes for an extremely bitter tonic and is best sweetened with sugar or honey. As a home remedy, gentian should be taken only under the supervision of an experienced herbalist. When taken in large doses, it can be toxic and will produce violent intestinal reactions. Early in this century gentian was a commercially significant plant, the root being used to flavor Moxie, a soft drink that was, in its day, almost as popular as Coca-Cola. Gentian is still cultivated commercially. It is an essential ingredient in vermouth and is a very popular medicinal in Europe. It is also the main ingredient in a popular French aperitif called *souze*. If you want to plant gentian as an ornamental, you must be patient; at least two seasons will pass before a young plant will flower.

Gentian Digestive Tonic

½ cup fresh gentian root
¼ cup fresh peppermint leaves
1 tablespoon fresh gingerroot, peeled and sliced
1 cup water
1 cup glycerin

Combine water and glycerin in a saucepan and simmer all ingredients over low flame for about 45 minutes. Strain. When liquid is cool, store in an amber jar or bottle. Take one teaspoon before each meal to aid digestion. This tonic will keep for about a year on the shelf and longer, when refrigerated.

GERMANDER

Teucrium chamaedrys

PERENNIAL

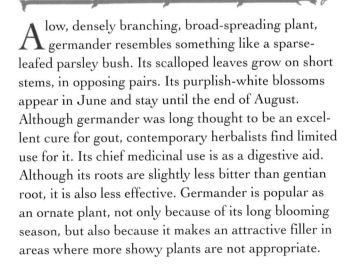

A low, densely branching, broad-spreading plant, germander resembles something like a sparse-leafed parsley bush. Its scalloped leaves grow on short stems, in opposing pairs. Its purplish-white blossoms appear in June and stay until the end of August. Although germander was long thought to be an excellent cure for gout, contemporary herbalists find limited use for it. Its chief medicinal use is as a digestive aid. Although its roots are slightly less bitter than gentian root, it is also less effective. Germander is popular as an ornate plant, not only because of its long blooming season, but also because it makes an attractive filler in areas where more showy plants are not appropriate.

GINGER

Zingiber officinale

    PERENNIAL

This much-prized spice plant is cultivated commercially in tropical regions throughout the world. Its distinctive rhizome, a bulbous, gnarly root complex, issues a single stalk of stemless green blades. Though we don't often think of ginger as a flowering plant, its blossoms are unusually attractive. Their pastel greenish-yellow base shades to a deep purple at the lips' edges. Both in the East and in the West, ginger has a long and honored history. Chinese herbalists were lauding its medicinal powers more than 3,000 years ago. Gingerroot is still considered by the Chinese to be an excellent stomachic, a cure for menstrual cramps and headaches, and an antidote for food poisoning as well. The ancients in the West also used ginger as a digestive aid. Ginger continues today to be used as an effective digestive aid, and is also known to be useful in lowering cholesterol, and bringing down high blood pressure. While ginger is a cardinal ingredient in many Chinese dishes, it has a place in the Western kitchen as well. Its popularity seems to be on the rise, and it is increasingly called for in contemporary American cooking. Homemade ginger ale, made from fresh gingerroot, tastes far superior to the store-bought swill and is remarkably easy to prepare. If you want to cultivate ginger, and you do not live in California, or one of the Gulf states, you'll need to build yourself a greenhouse. Ginger requires a tropical climate, with full sun and plenty of humidity.

For the Morning After

Gingerroot tea is an excellent hangover cure. It also relieves morning sickness.

GINKGO
Ginkgo biloba

Maidenhair tree

PERENNIAL

This tree is much treasured by the Chinese, who have cultivated it for thousands of years. The ginkgo is a tall tree, and a long-lived one. Some living trees are known to be more than a 1,000 years old. Ginkgo is easily identified by its distinctive leaves, triangular in form, with a scalloped outer edge. Flowers are tiny white buds. The fruit, well known for its rancid odor, is borne only by the female tree. Ginkgo berries have found a valued place for themselves in modern medical research. Some of its constituent elements have proved to be useful for enhancing memory functions. Ginkgo seems to act on the brain by increasing the circulation of blood. For this reason it seems to be effective in treating some of the symptoms of Alzheimer's disorder. Other medical uses for ginkgo are currently being researched, and it may well prove itself to be much more than just a landscaping tree. The ginkgo is often chosen as a landscape tree because it is distinctive, and because it is rather attractive when it flowers. Ginkgoes also make successful standards, and will not grow beyond a manageable size when stunted in a pot. Always select a male ginkgo at the nursery—it is the female that bears the fruit, which falls in autumn and fills the air with the fetid smell of rotting garbage.

Cure #2005 (It Works!)

Dill-seed tea is a reliable hiccup cure. Steep one teaspoon of dill seeds in a cup of boiling water for ten minutes, then drink it.

GINSENG

Panax ginseng, Panax schinseng, Panax quinque-folius, Eleutherococcus senticosus

Asiatic ginseng, Ren Shen, little men, man root, American ginseng, cinquefoil, five-fingers, red berry

PERENNIAL

This unusual plant sends up a single stem which branches only at the top, where it terminates in several radials of compound leaves. Its small five-petaled flowers first appear after three growing seasons, and only if conditions are right. Ginseng's famous root, a bulbous, gnarly rhizome, can take on virtually any form. Ginseng is native to the northeastern United States, where it grows wild in shaded, wooded areas.

Since the beginning of recorded history, ginseng has been the Chinese's most cherished root. The Chinese still believe ginseng to be a natural panacea, able to cure virtually anything, from digestive problems to a depressed mood. It is largely on account of ginseng's putative medicinal powers that it is cultivated so widely, and traded in Asia like a crop of gold, fetching astonishing prices on the open market. The Chinese value wild ginseng more highly than the cultivated plant, and in some regions of the Northeast, it is still gathered from the backwoods, from where it makes its way to the Chinese market. (Gathering has done significant damage to the native population of ginseng, and like other threatened species, it should be left to grow if seen in the wild.) Interestingly, many Native American tribes esteemed the ginseng root as having many of the same sacred and medicinal properties that were recognized by the Chinese.

Ginseng has limited culinary uses in Chinese cuisine. As an ingredient in soups, it is more likely intended to give the soup medicinal qualities, rather than to add flavor.

Ginseng can be cultivated by the amateur herbalist, but it requires patience and work. Sowing from seed is complicated; it is best to start with a first-year rootlet. Plant it in a shady, wooded spot, in rich soil. Do what you can to protect the root from vermin, especially gophers, who love ginseng. If you're lucky, you can pull a young, but mature, plant after four seasons.

GOLDENROD

Solidago virga-aurea, Solidago odora, Solidago cal-ifornica

Sweet-scented goldenrod, blue mountain tea

PERENNIAL

This common meadow grass is often seen growing in fields along the roadside. Regarded by most gardeners as one of the worst nuisance weeds, others appreciate its late-summer beauty, and let it flourish in their gardens. There are more than 100 varieties of goldenrod. Most of these are characterized by a tall, straight stem, terminating in dense clusters of tiny yellow flowers, lined along small terminal branches. Leaves are alternate, usually blade shaped and stemless. Different varieties of goldenrod are reputed to have different medicinal properties. The common varieties are said to make good astringents and to work well as a poultice on wounds. Goldenrod's putative healing powers have not been substantiated by contemporary research. If you're willing to classify goldenrod as a flowering ornamental (and you're not allergic to its pollen), plant it in dry, sandy soil, where it will get plenty of sun. Goldenrod makes an excellent building block for many herbal crafts. Be sure to shake the plant well after it's been properly dried.

GOLDENSEAL

Hydrastis canadensis

Yellow root, turmeric, orange root, yellow puccoon, eye balm, ground raspberry, jaundice root, Indian paint

PERENNIAL

This much sought-after herb is native to the eastern United States, and grows wild only in the most secluded spots in backwood forests. It is a small plant with large, broad, lobed leaves, resembling an irregularly shaped maple leaf. Both leaves and stem are covered with downy fibers. Goldenseal's short flower stems support pastel-green blossoms with prominent stamens. The flowers bloom in early spring and are followed by a cluster of small orange berries. Among some herbal enthusiasts goldenseal has a reputation that parallels ginseng's. It is used to cure every imaginable sort of digestive problem, as well as a wide variety of dermatological problems. Goldenseal's reputation is not a recent development; 19th-century-American folk herbalists believed that goldenseal was a virtual panacea. While there is no strong evidence that goldenseal has any real medicinal use at all, some research suggests that it may help to lower blood cholesterol. Goldenseal can usually be found in powdered form at the local health-food shop, but neither processed, nor fresh goldenseal should be taken in large doses, since it can be toxic. Like ginseng, goldenseal is extremely difficult to sow from seed. Those who want to cultivate their own are advised to start from a budded rootlet. Also like ginseng, goldenseal requires at least three to four seasons before you can pull a harvestable root.

Curry Cure!

If you have arthritis, eat curry. Turmeric, one of the key curry seasonings, relieves arthritis pain.

GOLDENTHREAD

Coptis groenlandica, Coptis trifolia

Mouth root, goldthread, canker root, yellow root, tisavoyanne

  PERENNIAL

This delicate creeping perennial is native to the northern United States and Canada. It can be found growing in densely wooded swampland, where the soil is dark and boggy. The tripartite leaves sit atop separate stems, as do the fine yellow-white flowers, which bloom from May through July. Goldenthread is reputed to be useful for the relief of canker sores and stomach ulcers, but it cannot be cultivated without the moisture and humidity supported by a greenhouse. It can, however, be gathered wild in many rural regions in the North. Herbalists who gather goldenthread for medicinal purposes do their hunting in September and October.

GOPHER PURGE

Euphorbia lathyris

Caper spurge, myrtle spurge

  ANNUAL, BIENNIAL

Gopher purge takes its name, as might be imagined, from its reputed ability to repel gophers. This single-stem plant grows straight upward, to a height of two to three feet. Its leaves are alternating and blade shaped, with rounded edges. Yellow flowers bloom in June, at the ends of short flower stems. Gopher purge has been used in the past among folk herbalists as a purgative, but is too violent and toxic for contemporary use. Its primary use now is as an ornate plant and a gardening tool. While some gardeners are uncertain as to its ability to turn away gophers, others swear by it. Since gopher purge is attractive when blooming, easy to sow and maintain, those gardeners who are plagued by gophers will find it a worthwhile experiment to build a "fence" of gopher purge around their most valuable plants.

GOTU KOLA
Centella asiatica

Gota kola, Brahmi

 PERENNIAL

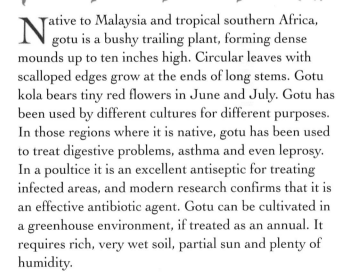

Native to Malaysia and tropical southern Africa, gotu is a bushy trailing plant, forming dense mounds up to ten inches high. Circular leaves with scalloped edges grow at the ends of long stems. Gotu kola bears tiny red flowers in June and July. Gotu has been used by different cultures for different purposes. In those regions where it is native, gotu has been used to treat digestive problems, asthma and even leprosy. In a poultice it is an excellent antiseptic for treating infected areas, and modern research confirms that it is an effective antibiotic agent. Gotu can be cultivated in a greenhouse environment, if treated as an annual. It requires rich, very wet soil, partial sun and plenty of humidity.

GRINDELIA

Grindelia camporum, Grindelia robusa

Gum plant, gumweed, scaly grindelia, rosinweed

    PERENNIAL

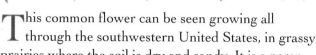

This common flower can be seen growing all through the southwestern United States, in grassy prairies where the soil is dry and sandy. It is a perennial, though the roots often fail after the first year.

GRINDELIA

Growing 20 inches high, *Grindelia comporum* has a straight and rigid stem that terminates with a yellow flower, which exudes a yellow sticky sap. Grindelia has been used in the past to treat acute cases of bronchitis, but its effectiveness in this capacity is questionable. Some southwestern Native American tribes found it useful as a poultice for treating rashes caused by poison ivy and poison oak. As an ornamental, grindelia has little to recommend it. It will do well in soil that is too poor to support other plants, but it is not an attractive plant.

GROUND IVY

Glechoma hederacea

Ale hoof, gill-over-the-ground, cat's foot, haymaids, creeping Charlie, creeping Jenny, runaway robin, robin-run-in-the-hedge

PERENNIAL

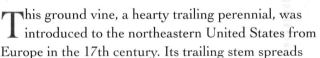

This ground vine, a hearty trailing perennial, was introduced to the northeastern United States from Europe in the 17th century. Its trailing stem spreads quickly and roots at regular intervals. The round, scalloped leaves have stems, as do the flowers, purplish coronet-shaped blossoms, which appear in June and July.

Ground ivy is sometimes called ale hoof, a name which dates to the 16th century, when this plant was cultivated for use in brewing beer.

European folk herbalists have used ground ivy in the past as an astringent for sore throats that are accompanied by an excess of phlegm. But contemporary herbalists have had little use for it and tend not to keep it in the garden, as it can be easily gathered in the wild.

Ground ivy can be used as a ground covering in wooded areas and is quite attractive in midsummer, but many gardeners will avoid planting it, since it spreads quickly and competes aggressively with other plants.

Herbal Insect Repellents

When you go camping or hiking, take a eucalyptus or geranium-based soap with you. The essential oils of these plants are excellent mosquito repellents.

GROUND PINE

Lycopodium complanatum

Trailing evergreen, ground cedar, Christmas green, creeping Jenny, club moss, snake moss, wolf's claw, lamb's tail, foxtail, hog's bed, stag's horn, vegetable sulfur

 PERENNIAL

The common name "ground pine" refers to the many varieties of the lycopod family, which is represented by at least one variety in virtually every temperate region of the world. This tiny creeping plant grows in boggy, wooded areas, where the soil is rich and wet. It takes its name from the shape of its leaves, narrow blades that form a radial spread, issuing from the terminus of a short stem. From a distance, the leaves look like pine needles. Having no flower, ground pine features a fruiting cap, which is covered with spore dust.

While the spore dust has limited medicinal use, it has an unusual ability to repel water. For this reason it can be used as a substitute for talcum powder, to prevent chafing in infants. The casual herbalist has little reason to cultivate ground pine, since it requires a greenhouse environment, and is by no means ornate.

HAWTHORN

Crataegus oxycantha, Crataegus monogyna

Mayflower, whitethorn, maybush, quickset

  PERENNIAL

The "mayflower tree" has been a favorite landscaping tree since ancient times, and for good reason. It brings color to the garden in every season, save for winter. Hawthorn's elegant white flowers bloom from May through June and are followed by clusters of bright red berries, which begin to appear at the end of July. The hawthorn is a good shade tree, with dense foliage and leaves that are somewhat maplelike. Hawthorn has become extremely valuable to the modern herbalist. Decoctions made from the fruit and the flower have proven to be useful in treating heart irregularities, having the effect of normalizing the heart's activity. Hawthorn is one of the most beautiful of trees and is unquestionably a satisfying landscaping medium. It can be grown from seed, but this is such a complicated and difficult process that one is best advised to buy a seedling from the nursery. Hawthorn likes to be in partial shade, among other trees, and in fairly rich soil.

HEMLOCK

Conium musculatum, Conium maculatum

Fool's parsley

PERENNIAL

This deadly poisonous plant, made famous by Plato's account of Socrates's death, was known to the ancient Greeks not only as a reliable killer, but as a medicinal as well. Hemlock is native to central and southern Europe, but has been naturalized to North America. It is a weedy-looking plant, with a slender, rigid stem and deeply divided, parsleylike leaves.

The stalk terminates in a floral umbel, whose radial branchlets support white florets.

Although hemlock has its medicinal purposes, it should only be used under strict medical supervision. Under no circumstances should the casual herbalist cultivate hemlock in the garden. Innumerable anecdotes tell of those who have mistaken hemlock's leaves for parsley (hence the name fool's parsley), or its tap for turnip. Ingestion of even the tiniest amount can induce vertigo. Larger amounts can easily be fatal.

HERB PARIS

Paris quadrifolia

PERENNIAL

Herb Paris is a common bog weed, which is native to all of central Europe, and parts of North America as well. Found growing in marshy, wooded areas, Paris has a single, unbranched stem, about four inches high, which terminates in four blade-shaped leaves. The foul-smelling yellow flower which blossoms at the center of the terminus, is followed by a single black berry. Called simply "herb" in medieval times, Paris was often mixed with wine because it was thought to be an aphrodisiac. The contemporary herbalist knows it to be highly toxic and finds no medicinal use for it. Paris has little to recommend it as ground cover, especially since it fills the air with a vaguely rank odor during the flowering season.

HOLLY

Ilex aquifolum, Ilex cassine, Ilex glabra, Ilex verticillata, Ilex vomitoria

Dahoon holly, yaupon, inkberry, gallberry, winterberry, black alder, prinos, fever bush, red-berried alder

    PERENNIAL

There are three varieties of holly and all of these are native to the eastern regions of North America. All are shrubs, found growing in marshy, wooded areas.

Holly is characterized by its thick, leathery, serrated leaves and its clusters of winterberries.

Glabra, or "inkberry," is a low-growing bush, with a black berry that gives it its common name. *Cassine*, or "dahoon holly," was used by some Native American tribes during ceremonies, to induce a mildly narcotic state. *Verticillata*, or "winterberry," is the common holly that is traditionally gathered during the holidays to make Christmas wreaths.

Although none of these varieties has any substantiated medicinal uses, winterberry used to be a staple remedy among folk herbalists, who used it as an astringent for the treatment of diarrhea. However, both the leaves and the berries are toxic, and holly has no place in the casual herbalist's medicine cabinet.

Winterberry lends itself especially well to herbal crafting, and its use for that purpose need not be limited to the holiday season.

HONEYSUCKLE

Lonicera caprifolium, Lonicera dioica

Italian honeysuckle, Italian woodbine

PERENNIAL

This ideal trellis-climber adds to the garden not only the beauty of its delicate yellow blossom, but it also fills the midsummer air with its sweet and pleasing scent. The honeysuckle blossom appears in early spring, a coronet-shaped yellow flower whose petals flare and turn back at the ends. Prominent stamens are a distinguishing characteristic of the flower. Honeysuckle's leaves are simple, stemless and rounded, almost circular. Indigenous to central Asia, and native to central Europe, the most common varieties of honeysuckle were long ago introduced to North America.

Over the centuries the Chinese have found medicinal uses for honeysuckle, most often using it to treat fevers. But Western herbalists have only rarely found a place for it as a medicinal, sometimes using it to treat asthma.

Honeysuckle's true appeal lies in its ornate charisma. Italian woodbine, the most common variety, is ideally planted around the porch or deck, where summer socializing is done. It is an agile climber, and will make its way quickly up a fence or a hedge. From the beginning of June, well into August, your porch will be graced with honeysuckle's potent, sweet fragrance.

HOP
Humulus lupulus

PERENNIAL

Hop is a climbing vine that is similar to the grapevine, save for its flower and its fruit. Native to central Europe and cultivated throughout Europe and North America, hop bears an inconspicuous white flower in June, which is followed on the female plant with a unique fruit, which is a shell of tiled, leaflike plates.

Hops have been a commercially significant crop plant since early in the 19th century. The fruit of the female plant is a valued constituent in the beer-brewing process.

Hops make hearty trellis vines, but as ornate plants, they do not come highly recommended. They are generally cultivated only by the most serious of home brewers.

HOREHOUND

Marrubium vulgare

Hoarhound, white horehound

  PERENNIAL

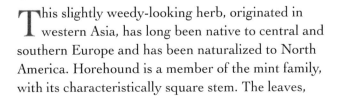

This slightly weedy-looking herb, originated in western Asia, has long been native to central and southern Europe and has been naturalized to North America. Horehound is a member of the mint family, with its characteristically square stem. The leaves, which come in opposing pairs at regular intervals along the stem, are covered with a downy fuzz. Tiny white flowers appear in clusters at each leaf axle.

Horehound has a long and illustrious history as a medicinal. The ancients ascribed to it a litany of remedial abilities so lengthy and various that they could rightly call this herb a panacea. In more recent centuries Europeans have concentrated on its demonstrated effectiveness as an excellent expectorant and cough suppressant. Homemade cough drops and cough syrup made from horehound have been a common answer to a sore throat since the early 17th century. Even today the English and the Germans keep alive this venerable tradition, making their own horehound cough-drop confections, using honey and marshmallow.

Horehound is a common fixture in the casual herbalist's garden; it sows from seed easily. It prefers sandy soil and will grow in full sun or partial shade.

HORSERADISH

Armoracia rusticana, Armoracia lapathifolia

PERENNIAL

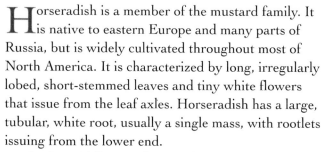

Horseradish is a member of the mustard family. It is native to eastern Europe and many parts of Russia, but is widely cultivated throughout most of North America. It is characterized by long, irregularly lobed, short-stemmed leaves and tiny white flowers that issue from the leaf axles. Horseradish has a large, tubular, white root, usually a single mass, with rootlets issuing from the lower end.

In the Middle Ages horseradish was more commonly used as a medicinal than as a condiment and was thought to be an effective diuretic. The inverse is true, today, and horseradish finds a place in the kitchen, where it is used as a culinary accent in many northern cuisines. Germans, Russians and Americans are especially keen on this herb and use it as a common condiment. Horseradish is the perfect complement to cold-meat platters and will add zing to just about any creamy salad dressing. Because it turns bitter quickly, it is best prepared fresh. A simple preparation is made by mixing the grated root with enough vinegar to leave it lumpy—not soupy. Mayonnaise can be added to tone down horseradish's potent bite.

Sowing horseradish from seed is a complicated process, but it can easily be grown from root cuttings. Plant horseradish in full sun, and give it rich, wet soil that has been heavily composted.

HORSETAIL

Equisetum arvense

Shavegrass, pewterwort, bottlebrush, jointweed, shavebrush, devil's guts, scouring rush

ANNUAL

Arvense is the most common of several varieties of horsetail, which are native to North America. The most distinguishing of its many unusual characteristics is its two-stage growth pattern. Horsetail begins as a single, tapering, bamboolike stalk, which terminates in a flower column, covered with very tiny white florets. In its second incarnation horsetail grows its namesake leaves — branching, bushy and needle shaped.

Horsetail has no culinary or medicinal uses, but it has a well-earned reputation among campers and outdoors people as a natural scouring cleaner. The stalks are rich with silica, a natural abrasive that will put a shine on pots and pans.

Horsetail spreads so vigorously that few gardeners will plant it, fearing they will lose control of it. But it is easily gathered in the wild, where it grows in boggy, shaded areas.

HYDRANGEA

Hydrangea arborescens

Seven barks, wild hydrangea

PERENNIAL

This well-known ornamental is distinguished by its flower, which forms a spherical cluster of florets that looks like a delicate snowball from a distance. Native throughout North America, a mature hydrangea bush may grow as high as ten feet and will bloom throughout July and August. Its flowers are usually white, but may shade to pink or blue, depending on the soil.

Native Americans often turned to the root and the bark of hydrangea as a diuretic, though its contemporary medicinal use is limited to the treatment of inflamed prostates.

Hydrangea earns its place in the garden as an ornamental bush. Its size, its density and its low-maintenance requirements make it an excellent landscaping tool. Use hydrangea to fill large spaces, and to serve as a colorful backdrop. Plant it in rich, slightly wet soil, where it will have full sun or partial shade.

HYSSOP

Hyssopus officinalis

PERENNIAL

This attractive flowering herb is native to central and southern Europe and parts of Asia, but has been native to North America since its introduction by

Hyssop

the earliest settlers. A member of the mint family, hyssop has mint's square stem, as well as its aromatic qualities. Its crushed leaves will issue a potent scent, which is minty, but also slightly acrid. Hyssop is characterized by a tall branching stem and opposing stemless leaves, which issue from axles in groups of four and five. Delicate blue flowers with prominent stamens cluster at the terminus, and at the upper leaf axles.

While herbalists of the past professed hyssop's effectiveness as a purgative, the modern herbalist finds only limited external uses for this plant, sometimes adding it to complex poultices, which are designed to promote the healing of wounds.

Hyssop is an excellent candidate for the beginning herbalist's garden. It is easily sown from seed and is remarkably resistant to pests and blight. Hyssop requires full sun, but the soil need not be especially rich.

ICELAND MOSS
Cetraria islandica

Iceland lichen, cetraria

 PERENNIAL

Although its amorphous "leaves" may give Iceland moss the appearance of an ordinary plant, it is not. A member of the lichen family, it is the product of a symbiotic joining of a fungus and algae. Like all lichens, Iceland moss anchors itself to a stationary base, usually a rock, and takes its moisture from the air. This particular lichen is native to North America, where it is found growing in wet and densely wooded areas.

Few among the many species of lichens have medicinal applications, but Iceland moss is one of the few. It contains a starchy substance that dissolves in boiling water and then gels upon cooling. This gelatinous preparation is said to be excellent for enhancing the appetite.

Iceland moss can be gathered in the wild, but like mushrooms, it must never be gathered except by those who are knowledgeable and experienced.

IRIS

Iris florentina, Iris germanica, Iris pallida

Orris root

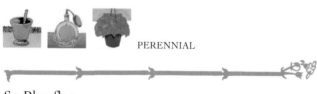

PERENNIAL

See Blue flag

JIMSONWEED

Datura stramonium

Jamestown weed, datura, stramonium, apple of Peru, thorn apple, stinkweed, devil's trumpet, angel's trumpet

PERENNIAL

This highly toxic plant originated in central Asia but is now native to Europe and North America. It can be identified by its irregularly dentate leaves, conical yellow or green flowers and an unusual fruit, which is an inch in diameter and covered with spines.

Jimsonweed is an aromatic plant, but its scent is anything but sweet; when the leaves are broken or crushed, the oils will issue an especially rank odor. Although jimsonweed has several useful medicinal applications, it does not belong in the amateur herbalist's cabinet. It is an hallucinogen, and it is deadly poisonous. The only feature that jimsonweed has that recommends its cultivation is its showy flower. If you have children, you should not have this plant in your garden.

JUNIPER
Juniperus communis

Common juniper, ground juniper, juniper bush, horse savin

PERENNIAL

This much-used landscaping bush represents a genus that includes over 40 varieties of evergreens. The most common of these is a dense, rambling shrub, which grows low to the ground. Some varieties grow upward, reaching a height of 25 feet. Juniper flowers in early spring, bearing tiny yellow or white florets. The winterberries are a deep shade of blue, almost purple.

Most people know that gin is produced through the distillation of juniper, but few know that juniper also has uses in the kitchen. The edible berry is too strongly flavored to eat raw, but it will add an appealing zing to meat and poultry dishes when used sparingly. Many folk recipes call for a few crushed juniper berries to be cooked with meat or fowl.

Juniper has earned an excellent reputation as a landscaping tree and provides the added benefit of filling your yard with its pleasant aroma. If you buy saplings from a nursery, be sure you know which variety you are getting—some grow outward, others grow upward.

Homemade Bath Oils

You can make bath oils for yourself, or as gifts. Simply take three parts mineral oil (available in most drug stores) and mix with one part essential oil of your favorite scented herb. Use peppermint or eucalyptus oil for an enervating bath, lavender for a calming one. Experiment with different oils for different moods.

KOLA
Cola nitida

PERENNIAL

The kola plant is indigenous to Africa, where it was valued as a medicinal herb long before the Europeans arrived on the continent. In the early 18th century, it was introduced to the Caribbean, and from there it found its way into the cabinets of American herbalists and pharmacists. In Africa and in the Caribbean, the kola bean was chewed as a stimulant and was known also for its ability to relieve bronchial congestion. Before the 1930s, American pharmacists prescribed a kola syrup for the relief of asthma. It was just before the turn of the century that the world's most famous soft drink was invented by mixing kola syrup with carbonated water. Although the popularity of cola soft drinks may be due in part to the caffeine "rush" they provide, kola beans have much less natural caffeine than coffee beans. Most commercial cola drinks are "fortified" with added caffeine.

Protect and Preserve

Dried herbs, extracts and tinctures keep best when stored in colored-glass bottles away from direct sunlight. You can save the amber-glass jars and bottles that vitamins come in, and store herbs in them, or you can buy tinted-glass jars or bottles from an herb-crafting supply company. Not only do these tinted-glass jars keep herbs safe from light, they look lovely on your spice rack.

LADY'S SLIPPER

Cypripedium calceolus, Cypripedium pubescens,
Cypripedium acaule

Nerve root, American valerian, moccasin flower

PERENNIAL

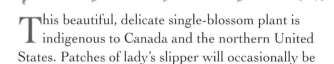

This beautiful, delicate single-blossom plant is indigenous to Canada and the northern United States. Patches of lady's slipper will occasionally be

seen, growing among marshy grasses at the edge of a forest. But lady's slipper has become an endangered species, and it must never be gathered in the wild. If this plant's natural existence has been threatened by over gathering, it is easy to understand why. It is an unusually elegant plant, with lily like, bladed leaves surrounding a bright yellow, orchidlike blossom, which is exquisite.

Tinctures made from lady's slipper were one a common remedy for anxiety, and it was thought to be an excellent natural sedative. But the best reason to make this plant part of your garden, is its exotic elegance. Lady's slipper will thrive in moist, heavily composted soil. It is also adaptable to planters and pots, so long as it is watered regularly and has good drainage. Remember that lady's slipper must be purchased from the nursery and never gathered from the wild.

LAMB'S EARS

Stachys byzantina

Woundwort, woolly betony

PERENNIAL

Lamb's ears are called so because of its fuzzy grayish-green leaves. They make a perfect addition to any garden, especially if you have children. This plant is harmless and children enjoy the texture of the leaves. It grows well in full sun or shade, in just about any soil, and makes a lovely border plant. It flowers in late spring, with lovely pink or purple blooms. The leaves can be steamed or sautéed, or tossed into a salad of field greens. Lamb's ears have a gentle flavor, although some people do not enjoy the texture. It does take some getting used to. The leaves can also be dried and made into a mild tea. Its medicinal uses are minor, but it has been used as a natural dressing to stop bleeding.

136

LAVENDER

Lavandula vera, Lavandula angustifolia,
Lavandula officinalis

English lavender

PERENNIAL

This long-stemmed wildflower is native to central and southern Europe, but is cultivated in many regions of the world. The three common species of lavender are characterized by long, slender leaves, issuing directly above the root complex, and a tall, straight woody stem, which terminates in a long cluster of lavender-colored florets.

The aromatic oils in this sweetly scented wildflower have been used for many centuries as a key ingredient in perfumes, as well as scented soaps and oils. In Europe lavender tea is considered a medicinal, and is taken for the calming effect it has on an upset stomach.

Plant lavender in your herb garden and you'll enjoy its sweet, fragrant scent during flowering months, from July to September. Dry the flowers in a cool, arid room; tie the dried petals into cheesecloth satchels, and place these in your linen closet and your clothes closets. The dried lavender will stay actively aromatic for many months.

Cool Those Aching Feet

To make a soothing footbath, add dried nettle leaves, lavender and lemon balm to boiling water in a bucket or plastic container large enough for both of your feet. Let the herbs steep until the water has cooled just enough to immerse your feet comfortably.

If you live in a less temperate region, and you'd like to plant lavender, be sure to cut it back for the winter, and insulate the roots with plenty of compost or mulch.

LEMON

Citrus limon

PERENNIAL

Lemon is a prized fruit and herb. It is a well-known folk remedy for congestion and phlegm, and an essential ingredient to the hot toddy. It is a good source of vitamin C. Its oil is used in many cosmetics and perfumes, as well as soaps, shampoos and astringents. It is a valuable culinary ingredient and flavors desserts, main dishes, beverages, candies and sauces. If you live in Florida or California, you may be able to grow a lemon tree in your garden. Make sure it has lots of sun and sufficient water. It is a beautiful tree, with a sweet aroma.

LEMON BALM

Melissa officinalis

Common balm, honey plant, dropsy plant, citronele

PERENNIAL

Lemon balm is a member of the mint family, with its characteristic square stem and opposing jagged-edged leaves. It is native to southern Europe, but was long ago naturalized to many different parts of the world, including the more temperate regions of North

America, where it was introduced by the early colonists. Late in the summer lemon balm's yellow-white florets bloom at the base of the leaf axles.

For many centuries lemon balm was valued in Europe for its mild, tranquilizing effect. Contemporary scientific investigations indicate that a belief in balm's sedative effects is not at all unfounded.

The contemporary herbalist's chief uses for balm are in the kitchen, and as an aromatic. Fresh balm leaves mix nicely with other greens in a garden salad. It is also a common ingredient in potpourris, lending its potent lemony scent to just about any mix of scented herbs.

Lemon balm is not an ornamental plant, with its scraggly, jagged leaves. But it has its place in the herbal garden; a single plant will yield more than enough leaves for plenty of mild lemony tea.

LEMON VERBENA

Verbena citriodora, Aloysia triphylla

Cedron

PERENNIAL

L emon Verbena is a native of the foothills of the Andes Mountains. Its name comes from the sweet lemonscent of its leaves and pale lavender flowers. It has limited medicinal use, but makes a pleasant infusion that can alleviate nausea and indigestion. Its essential oils are used in making perfume. Its dried leaves and flowers make excellent additions to a citrus potpourri. Cedron is gaining popularity as a culinary herb and can be used in any recipe that calls for lemongrass or lemon thyme. It is often used in pastry baking and fruit recipes, but it is finding its way into savory recipes as well. Lemon-verbena tea is delicious and quite refreshing when served iced. Since lemon verbena is a tropical native, it does not grow well outdoors in North America. However, it is a good potherb and will flourish indoors in a warm spot with lots of sunshine.

LEMONGRASS
Cymbopogon citratus

      PERENNIAL

This tall grass, with its long, spindly, gradually attenuated leaves, is indigenous to the wet and temperate regions of Indochina, where it is cultivated commercially on a large scale. Lemongrass takes its name from the strong, citruslike scent that issues from the sap of its leaves. The lemony oil is used commercially to flavor a variety of food products, soaps and perfumes.

In the Philippines and Thailand, lemongrass is an essential ingredient in some of these cultures' most popular dishes.

Lemongrass tea is used medicinally by cultures throughout the world to treat digestive problems, as well as the symptoms of fever.

If you live in any of the Gulf states, you can easily grow lemongrass in your herb garden. Use it in teas; use it to add zing to soups, and blend its oil into candles to create a natural and effective mosquito repellent. Lemongrass is not pretty to look at, so plant it in a less conspicuous area of your garden.

Herbal Insect Repellents

Planting these herbs in your garden will help repel unwanted insect pests:

Anise	Marigold
Catnip	Nasturtium
Eucalyptus	Pyrethrum
Fennel	Rue
Lemongrass	Tansy

LICORICE
Glycyrrhiza glabra

PERENNIAL

The root of this small tree has lent its unique taste to sweets and to special dishes for more than 2,000 years. Licorice is indigenous to the Mediterranean, but has been naturalized in many parts of the world, including California. The average licorice tree grows to a height of four feet, and issues from a massive, knobby, bulbous root complex.

Licorice has been valued for thousands of years, both in Europe and the Middle East, not only as a natural sweetener, but also as a medicinal with a remarkable repertoire of curative effects. Among licorice root's putative powers are included the promotion of menstruation, the healing of ulcers, and the quieting of upset stomachs.

Today licorice is cultivated primarily for use in making sweets and tobacco products. Its chief medicinal use is as an ingredient in commercial cough syrups and expectorants.

Licorice candies produced in this country were generally authentic until the 1960s, when manufacturers began simulating the licorice flavor with counterfeit ingredients. Our older generations may recall that licorice sticks used to have a much more potent taste, with a unique sweetness.

Unless you live in southern California, or a similarly warm, dry climate, including a licorice among your landscape trees is not advisable. They are difficult to plant from seedling and difficult to maintain.

LIFE ROOT

Senecio vulgaris

Groundsel, ragwort

PERENNIAL

L ife root and ragwort are the common names for the many species in this family of herbs, which is distantly related to the thistles. Most varieties are characterized by a tall stem, sparsely foliated with two distinct leaf types. The radial leaves are simple and ovate — almost circular. The upper leaves are spear shaped, with dented edges. The long, straight stem terminates in a branching crown, the shoots of which each support a cluster of florets. Life root flowers in the early spring. It has been naturalized to many regions around the world, and in this country, is native to the eastern states, where it grows in loamy soil, usually on the banks of streams and rivers.

Although life root is a valued player in the professional herbalist's repertoire of herbs, it should not be used by the amateur. When taken in large doses, life root is toxic. The serious herbalist will keep life root in her garden, but it has a "weedy" look, and does not make an attractive ornate plant.

LILY OF THE VALLEY

Convallaria majalis

Convallaria, May lily, Our Lady's tears

PERENNIAL

At one time lily of the valley was considered an official drug, not only as a substitute for digitalis, but for many other uses. However, lily of the valley is poisonous. It does make a fragrant and pretty contribution to an ornamental garden.

LOVAGE
Levisticum officinale

PERENNIAL

L ovage is a perennial herb that looks and tastes very much like celery. Its thick, straight, ribbed stalk branches only at its end, around which the small, jagged-edged leaves are clustered. Lovage is native to North America, and to Europe, where it was cultivated in centuries past as a stock vegetable.

Lovage also has a long history in southern Europe as a medicinal herb. It was used for many centuries to soothe an upset stomach and was thought to promote menstruation.

Today lovage's fundamental place is in the kitchen. The leaves can be used in salads, and the chopped stems make an excellent filler in soups and stews. Like celery, it brings out the flavor of more strongly flavored meats and vegetables.

Lovage is an excellent candidate for the low-maintenance vegetable garden. Sow it from seed in a sunny spot with rich soil, and this perennial will return each summer with barely any attention at all.

LUNGWORT
Pulmonaria officinalis

Jerusalem cowslip, lung plant

PERENNIAL

L ungwort is a broad-leaved ground cover indigenous to central European woodlands and now native to the northeastern states in this country. It can be recognized by its foot-long leaves, which issue from short stems, directly above the roots. The leaves are mottled with lungwort's characteristic patches of white. Conical, purplish-blue flowers appear in April and May.

Lungwort takes its name from its reputed ability to relieve a variety of respiratory problems. In the Middle Ages it was commonly used to treat bronchial congestion. In Russia it continues to be used as a folk-remedy for the same purpose.

Although lungwort's curative powers have never been substantiated, there is no question that it makes an excellent landscaping plant. The broad leaves form an elegant, dense ground cover in partially wooded areas where the soil is rich and moist. The early blossoms will provide plenty of color before other flowering plants have bloomed.

MADDER

Rubia tinctorum

Madder root, Turkey red

PERENNIAL

Madder is a perennial, which is indigenous to southern Europe and parts of Asia. It was introduced to North America in the 16th century, but it has become native only in southern regions. It is a climbing herb, which cannot support itself. Madder's stem is lined with tiny climbing stalks that allow it to adhere to other plants as it grows upward. This plant bears very tiny, conical flowers in May and June. Madder was much used as a medicinal by the Greeks, who believed it could relieve many problems related to the urinary tract and menstruation. Modern herbalists, however, have few, if any, uses for this herb. Until the 20th century, madder was a commercially significant plant, used by fabric mills in England as a dye for both wool and cotton. Its history as a dyestuff dates back to the ancients, who used the natural alizarin found in madder root to give a bright red highlight to their garments. Herbalists with an interest in dyeing clothing and fabric by hand will make a place for madder in their gardens. Because it is the roots from which the dye is made, the plant must be given plenty of room for the roots to spread. Madder does best when it has an appropriate host plant (or chicken wire) on which to climb. Hand-dyeing with madder is a complicated process. Those interested in using madder root to create their own dyes, should consult reference works that deal with natural dyes.

MARJORAM

Origanum vulgare, Origanum majorana

Pot marjoram, sweet marjoram

PERENNIAL

This mainstay of the herbal garden has many uses. Not only is it an essential kitchen herb, it also has a significant place in the European folk-herbalist tradition.

The three most common varieties of marjoram (wild, sweet and potted) are all similar in both flavoring and appearance. Marjoram has a look and a taste that is vaguely like oregano. Marjoram's long green stalk, which terminates in an upward sweep of radial florets, looks something like an umbrella turned inside out by the wind. The delicate, stringy leaves hang in clusters from axles along the stalk. Wild marjoram is most often used in medicinals. The mild tea of the wild marjoram leaf is reputed to be a sedative, good for

relieving tension-related headaches. Sweet marjoram is
an essential kitchen herb for French, Portuguese and
Italian cuisine, and it makes an excellent complement
to rosemary on roasts and in stews. Marjoram grows
well in fully drained soil, but it needs to be tended with
care. Although it is a perennial, it is very difficult to
coax through a harsh northern winter. Some gardeners
will pot it before the second bloom and bring it indoors
for the winter. More often, marjoram is treated as an
annual, germinated from the seed in March and planted in late May to avoid the frosts. Marjoram's dried
floral crown adds an appealing touch to many herbal

crafts and has the added benefit of infusing a room with a subtle, sweet aroma—even after drying.

MARSH MARIGOLD

Caltha palustris

Cowslip, may-blob, palsywort, king cup

    PERENNIAL

The marsh marigold is a beautiful garden plant. Its showy yellow flowers, which look like giant buttercups, will lend dramatic beauty to any ornamental garden. It loves very moist soil and shade and opens and closes with the sun. The marsh marigold was a holy flower to the early pagans, and on May Day they hung garlands of may-blob over doorways. Later the Christians co-opted this idea and dedicated the marsh marigold to the Virgin Mary. Juice from this Eurasian native was used to cure warts topically. Infusions were thought to prevent fits. All parts of the marsh marigold contain irritating substances. It is not recommended that any part of the plant be ingested, and topical use should only be practiced under the supervision of a trained herbalist.

MARSHMALLOW

Althaea officinalis

Mortification root, sweet weed

      PERENNIAL

This is the plant that lends its name to the puffy sugar-candy that we toast over campfires on the end of sticks. But the marshmallow we buy in the supermarket won't list this plant among its many synthetic ingredients. The original marshmallow confection was prepared from the root of the plant, stripped of its hard outer skin, boiled and sugared. It had a spongy consistency something like its modern store-bought derivative.

It grows in full sun, in marshes and wet fields with humus-rich soil. A fast-growing perennial with long branching stems, it grows to a height of four feet or more. The large leaves are four inches long, lobed at the base, and jagged at the end.

Marshmallow flowers in July, bearing pinkish-white blossoms, which turn to fruits in August. The entire aerial portion of the plant dies back in October.

Marshmallow has a long history among Western cultures as both a culinary and a medicinal plant. The ancients used it as a common poultice on every sort of wound. From the time of the Greeks through the Middle Ages, marshmallow was a fall-back source of nourishment when crops were destroyed by locusts or drought. The young leaves are edible, and the root portion makes a substantial meal when boiled until soft, then fried in butter and onions.

Ease Your Tired Eyes

Chamomile soothes tired eyes. Simply take two chamomile tea bags, and dip them in cool water until completely saturated. Squeeze out excess liquid, and place one tea bag on each eye.

MATTÉ

Ilex paraguariensis

Jesuit tea, Yerba mate, Paraguay tea, hervea

  PERENNIAL

Matté is a fruit-bearing herb that is indigenous to South America. It was the Jesuit missionaries in South America who introduced the native Indians' favorite tea to the European colonists. In the past matté has never been very popular in North America, but is gaining popularity as a coffee substitute. It is a favorite brew of the Argentines and the Brazilians and has a high caffeine content.

MAYAPPLE

Podophyllum peltatum

American mandrake, wild jalap, hogapple, ground lemon, Indian apple, vegetable mercury, umbrella plant, duck's foot, vegetable calomel, yellowberry

  PERENNIAL

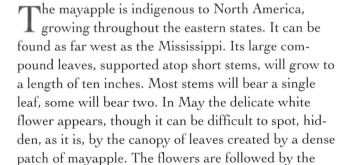

The mayapple is indigenous to North America, growing throughout the eastern states. It can be found as far west as the Mississippi. Its large compound leaves, supported atop short stems, will grow to a length of ten inches. Most stems will bear a single leaf, some will bear two. In May the delicate white flower appears, though it can be difficult to spot, hidden, as it is, by the canopy of leaves created by a dense patch of mayapple. The flowers are followed by the fruit, a yellow-green, oblong bulb, which is the only part of the plant that is edible. (Do not eat the poisonous seeds). Mayapple was used by Native Americans to eliminate warts, and its effectiveness in this capacity is well substantiated. At least one commercial product that is sold as a treatment for warts incorporates a derivative of the essential oils of mayapple.

However, the amateur herbalist is cautioned not to experiment with mayapple. Most of the plant, including the roots, are highly toxic, and have no internal uses. Even external applications to normal skin tissue can cause severe irritation. Mayapple makes an attractive addition to both the herb garden and the wildflower garden. It does particularly well in the shade and must be tended carefully since the rhizome will spread quickly in moist soil and tends to overtake other plants.

MEADOWSWEET

Filipendula ulmaria

Spirea

PERENNIAL

Meadowsweet is a perennial herb that is indigenous to Europe and was introduced to North America by colonists, probably in the 16th century. Its long, branching stem bears a maple-shaped leaf at the end of each stalk, and two spear-shaped opposing leaves, several inches below the terminal leaf. Meadowsweet blooms from June through August, and bears a dense, terminal cluster of tiny white florets. Before the 20th century meadowsweet's primary use was as an aromatic. The flowers have a strong, sweet bouquet and have long been used in Europe to mask unpleasant odors in the home. Dried petals were strewn on the floor and in cabinets, in every room in the house. In modern times meadowsweet has found more importance as a medicinal. This herb contains salicin and spirin, which are natural analgesics. In fact, the first aspirin produced by Bayer Pharmaceutical in the 19th century, was derived from meadowsweet. As a remedy for the aches and fever of a flu, a tincture made from meadowsweet offers slightly less effective relief than aspirin, but it will not cause stomach upset. Meadowsweet is the perfect border plant for a formal garden. Its stunning white flower clusters bloom all through the summer in full or partial sun. But meadowsweet does require some attention. It will grow only in rich, well-watered soil and it needs to be heavily composted, at least once each season.

MILKWEED

Asclepias syriaca

Common milkweed, silkweed

 PERENNIAL

This common perennial is indigenous to North America and is a familiar sight in marshy fields and waste places from Canada to Florida. The single stem bears oval leaves in opposing pairs and terminates in a cluster of tiny purple and white flowers. These are followed in August by a seedpod, which looks something like a hanging cocoon and is filled with white downy-haired seeds. Milkweed takes its name from its milky sap, which will seep out when the stem is cut or when a leaf is broken off. Milkweed has been used medicinally for everything from inducing abortions to treating bronchitis, but none of its properties has been substantiated. Many naturalists know that the young shoots, cut well above the roots and gathered in the spring, are edible and quite tasty. They have a strong flavor, vaguely like asparagus. (As with any wild plant, you should not harvest milkweed for the kitchen without consulting a knowledgeable naturalist. There are at least three varieties of milkweed, and not all are edible.) Milkweed does not make a satisfactory garden plant. Although the flowers are a beautiful shade of purple, the plant itself is gangly and sparse—not at all pleasant to look at. The herbalist who wants to make use of the leaf or the milk will likely find milkweed growing in the wild, no matter what region of the country she lives in.

MILK THISTLE

Silybum marianum

Variegated thistle, Our Lady's milk thistle

PERENNIAL

This common thistle is covered with tiny spines and bears a purple-violet flower in June and July. Milk thistle is indigenous to Italy and Greece and was brought to this country in the 17th century. It thrives in California, where it grows wild in dry, rocky soil. Milk thistle is not only edible, it was once cultivated in Europe as a stock vegetable. After the leaves have been trimmed of their prickly edges, they can be steamed or

Liver Protector

Before you go out on the town, swallow some milk-thistle capsules. Milk thistle helps promote a healthy liver by cleansing it of toxins. It may negate the damage you do by overindulging in alcohol.

sautéed. They must be heavily flavored, as they are bland, with a hint of bitterness. It is highly regarded as a liver tonic and can be found in capsule form in most natural-food stores. Few gardeners would plant this particular thistle among their herbs, and it is widely regarded as a nuisance weed. In fact, the beautiful purple flower, which blooms all through the summer, makes a nice addition to any wild garden. Milk thistle will grow in full and partial sun, in all kinds of soil, but should be watched carefully, as it spreads easily.

MINT

Mentha spp.

(Peppermint) *brandy mint, lamb mint, curled mint, balm mint;* (Orangemint) *bergamot mint, eau de cologne mint;* (Applemint) *round-leaved mint;* (Spearmint) *common garden mint, Lady's mint, mackerel mint, lamb mint, curly mint, Kentucky Colonel, pea mint*

PERENNIAL

The mint family (*Labiatae*) is large and diverse. Many of its members are included in this book as separate entries, since those particular mints are used for very different purposes than more common mints. It is possible to group some mints together, since their differences are subtle and their uses similar. In this group we have the most popular and well-known mint there is—peppermint *(M. x piperita)*. Peppermint is thought to be a hybrid of spearmint and watermint. It was recognized for its medicinal value centuries ago and continues to be used to treat digestive ailments, and as a tonic. It makes a soothing tea for an upset stomach and, combined with ginger, is an effective treatment for motion sickness. It is a common ingredient in many cosmetics and invigorating soaps. It is widely used in cooking and making candy. As a garden herb, it is superior. It is easy to grow in sun or shade

and will flourish outdoors or on a windowsill. Just
keep it well drained and moist, and it will give you
beautiful white or light purple flowers, and fresh mint
for your juleps, teas and jellies. It is best to cultivate
from cuttings. Orangemint *(M. Citrata or odorata)* is
another popular mint family member. Like peppermint,
it is easy to grow. Its leaves are tinged with purple and
it has lovely mauve flowers. Its strong aroma—a pleasing, lemony, minty odor—will permeate your garden. It
is not used medicinally, but can be used in teas, jellies
and any other place you would utilize peppermint. It
makes a wonderful addition to potpourri. Applemint

(M. Rotundifolia) is named such because of its applemint aroma. It is widely used as a kitchen herb in sweet and savory dishes. It is milder than other mints and can be used liberally. Like the other mints, it is easy to grow. It will give forth delicate white or pink flowers. Spearmint *(Mentha spicata)* is the most commonly used of all mints. Its name refers to the spear shape of the leaves. It is native to southern Europe, but is cultivated worldwide. Its uses are very similar to those of peppermint, and like the other mints, it is a pleasure to grow. New mint varieties are being hybridized every day. Lately we have seen pineapple mint *(Mentha suaveolens)* which, like applemint, is named for its pineapple aroma and flavor, and candy mint and chocolate mint. Japanese mint *(Mentha arvensis)* has been used for centuries to make menthol, and Corsican mint *(M. Requienii)* is the original flavor for crème de menthe.

MISTLETOE
Viscum album

PERENNIAL

Mistletoe is a tree-born evergreen shrub, making a home for itself in the branches of just about any variety of host tree. Its tiny green leaves are oblong, thick and leathery. Mistletoe flowers in May and June, blooming very tiny flowers. The white one-seeded berry is born later, appearing in September and October. Mistletoe grows throughout Europe and can be found in this country through most of the eastern states. Kissing under the mistletoe is a well-known tradition that dates back to pagan times. Pre-Christian Europe welcomed in the New Year with ceremonies that incorporated mistletoe. Like so many other pagan traditions, it was woven into the Christian tradition in the Middle Ages. Decoctions made from mistletoe were used by Native Americans to induce labor during childbirth and sometimes to induce abortion. Mistletoe remedies are rarely prescribed for any reason by modern herbalists and must never be experimented with in the home, as many mistletoe preparations are toxic.

MOTHERWORT

Leonurus cardiaca

Lion's tail, lion's ear, throwwort

PERENNIAL

M otherwort is a hearty, single-stem perennial with deep-toothed leaves. Growing to a height of four to five feet, motherwort flowers in May and June, bearing pink and white flowers along its terminal spikes.

It is an herb with a long medicinal tradition in Europe, dating back to the ancients. Not indigenous to America, it was introduced to this continent by the colonists.

Although many medicinal applications have been ascribed to motherwort over the centuries, it was best known to the ancients as an antidepressant, reputed to lift the spirits and ward off melancholy.

Contemporary herbalists recognize motherwort's mild sedative action and will also prescribe it as an antispasmodic, which is particularly useful in treating heart palpitations.

MUGWORT
Artemisia vulgaris

Sailor's tobacco, motherwort

PERENNIAL

Mugwort was introduced to this country from Europe, probably in the 17th century. In the northeastern states it can be found growing along the roadside and along riverbanks, in moist, rich soil. This perennial can grow from three to five feet in height, and bears a delicate, aromatic, branching leaf, the underside of which is covered with a downy white fuzz.

Mugwort was traditionally used to give a bitter flavoring in some liquors, including absinthe. In the 17th and 18th centuries, the English used this plant for brewing beer, and this may be the origin of its common name, although some writers have suggested that it more likely takes its name from *mothe*, Old English for moth. Mugwort is an effective repellent against wool-eating moths.

Although decoctions are traditionally prepared to soothe gastrointestinal problems and to promote men-

160

Mugwort

Repel Moths without the Moth Ball Odor

Dried mugwort discourages moths. Hang some in your closet mixed with some dried lavender and rosemary. It is an effective herbal repellent, as well as an air freshener. Take equal parts of each dried herb, and place them in the toe section of an old pair of stockings or panty hose. Tie with a ribbon or string, and hang in your closet, or place in your bureau drawers.

struation, the amateur herbalist should avoid prescribing mugwort. It can produce a potent and unpleasant narcotic effect and can cause a violent reaction unless taken in cautious moderation.

MULLEIN

Verbascum thapsus

Flannel flower, hage taper, common mullein, flannel plant, velvet dock, candlewick, Aaron's rod, lungwort, Adam's Flannel

BIENNIAL

Mullein is a biennial that bears a single, full-length stem every other year and an abbreviated stem in the years in between. The four-foot stem of the full plant bears foot-long, spear-shaped leaves and terminates in a flowering crown with deep yellow blossoms. The leaves are covered on both sides with a downy white fur. This is a hearty plant that can be found growing in just about every region throughout the United States, thriving in dry, sandy soil.

Mullein is considered by many herbalists to be an effective treatment for bronchitis and for many respiratory irritations. A decoction can be prepared from either the leaves or the flowers, although the flowers are considered more effective in treating bronchitis.

Amateur herbalists should be aware that the seeds of mullein are toxic and must never be included in preparations that are taken internally.

Mullein will make a nice addition to the herb garden and the flower garden alike, with its beautiful, deep-yellow spike of flowers, towering above smaller plants. But it requires thoughtful management, since it self-sows quickly and can easily get out of control.

MUSTARD

Brassica nigra, Brassica alba, Brassica napus

Black mustard, white mustard, false mustard

   PERENNIAL

Mustards are useful in the kitchen, sickroom and the garden. A mustard plaster or poultice is a "classic" folk cure for chest congestion. Mustard plasters can also be used to relieve arthritis and other inflammations. Mustard is also an appetite stimulant, but should be used with care. Ingesting too much mustard seed can cause stomach irritation and nausea. Mustard's popularity as a condiment goes back to ancient times. Ancient Greeks and Romans pulverized the seeds and mixed them with wine to make the precursor to our mustard. The whole seeds can be used in making pickles. Young mustard greens are delicious stir-fried or steamed, and they are good for you. Mustard is a satisfying plant to grow. In the early spring its delicate yellow flowers will let you know that summer is on its way. In the fall you can harvest the seeds and make your own homemade mustard. Mustard needs good soil and full sun.

MYRRH

Commiphora mol-mol

 PERENNIAL

The myrrh is a small tree, growing to an average height of four feet, with knotty, twisting branches, foliated with dark-green tripartite leaflets. Not native to America, myrrh grows almost exclusively in the Middle East, where it is found in sunny spots, with dry, sandy soil. This is the same myrrh that was brought by the three wise men to Christ's manger. It has been prized for many centuries as a precious oil, but it is not the leaves or the flowers that are so highly valued. Rather, it is myrrh's thick, amber, resinous sap that is used to derive the potent scented oil.

Over the millennia myrrh was most commonly sought as a perfumed body oil, but it is also used in soaps and as an ingredient in perfumes. In ancient times myrrh was used as an aromatic burning oil, giving a rich, pungent aroma to the temple or home that had a myrrh lamp.

SWEET
CICELY

Herbal Gum Repair

A tincture of myrrh will help heal a cold sore.
Apply to affected area with cotton swab at least
three times a day. Myrrh also promotes healthy
gums. Toothpaste and mouthwashes made with
myrrh are readily available at your natural-foods
store.

NASTURTIUM
Tropaeolum minus, Tropaeolum majus

   ANNUAL

This delicate, flowering vine is ideal for the small trellis, with its distinctive circular leaves, and its elegant, brightly colored blossom. Nasturtium is an especially satisfying fence-climber as it flowers throughout the summer, bearing its broad-petaled blossoms in yellow, orange or bright red.

Nasturtium is not just an ornate addition to the flower garden; both the leaves and the flower are edible. The latter makes a brightly ornate garnish in any garden salad.

Nasturtium will sow easily from seed, and does well in many soils, so long as it has full sun and enough water. In the flower garden, its bright blossom may compete with less showy flowers. Try planting it around the base of your porch (if you have one), and let it climb the fencing. Nasturtium's flower has an exquisitely sweet fragrance, which you'll enjoy on summer evenings.

NUTMEG

Myristica fragrans

Mace

 PERENNIAL

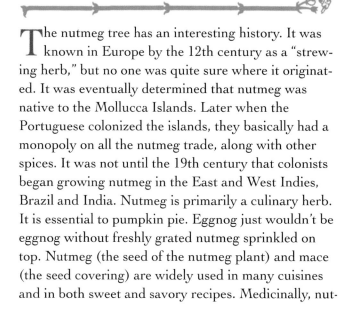

The nutmeg tree has an interesting history. It was known in Europe by the 12th century as a "strewing herb," but no one was quite sure where it originated. It was eventually determined that nutmeg was native to the Mollucca Islands. Later when the Portuguese colonized the islands, they basically had a monopoly on all the nutmeg trade, along with other spices. It was not until the 19th century that colonists began growing nutmeg in the East and West Indies, Brazil and India. Nutmeg is primarily a culinary herb. It is essential to pumpkin pie. Eggnog just wouldn't be eggnog without freshly grated nutmeg sprinkled on top. Nutmeg (the seed of the nutmeg plant) and mace (the seed covering) are widely used in many cuisines and in both sweet and savory recipes. Medicinally, nut-

meg is used in very small amounts to aid digestion and relieve flatulence. But be careful if you use nutmeg as a medicinal herb. Large amounts will cause hallucinations and possible convulsions. I strongly recommend you keep nutmeg in the kitchen. The nutmeg tree is not grown in North America.

An Herbal Treat For Your Skin

Many salons offer special herbal steam-cleansing for your face, but you can give yourself a steam "facial" at home. Boil four cups of water and place in a glass bowl. Add two tablespoons of dried chamomile and elderflowers (or any of your favorite dried herbs), place a towel over your head to cover your face, and lean over the bowl. Sit for about 15 minutes. The herbal steam will open your pores, and purify your skin. After 15 minutes, wipe your face with a cool, damp washcloth, and apply your favorite herbal mask. There are countless herbal masks, and you can make any kind you like using a thick base like yogurt, oatmeal and egg whites. Simply add your favorite herb, crushed, or herbal extract. I especially like an oatmeal mask made with witch hazel. It is cleansing and refreshing. Apply any herbal mask to your face, avoiding the eye areas, and sit for 15 minutes. Rinse off with warm water, and then apply an astringent or toner. Rose water makes a lovely and gentle toner. After toning, moisturize with your favorite moisturizer.

OATS

Avena sativa

Groats, oatstraw

ANNUAL

*A*vena is a member of the grass family and is widely cultivated commercially as a basic food staple. In the kitchen it is in oatmeal and oatmeal cookies. It can be used as a soup thickener. It is highly nutritious, loaded with fiber and protein. It is also a soothing medicinal herb. Externally, in a lotion or in a bath, oats can soothe skin irritations, especially shingles and chicken pox. Commercial preparations of colloidal oatmeal made specifically for the bath are available in any pharmacy. Taken internally, it is thought to be an antidepressant. There is not much evidence to support this, but it couldn't hurt.

Soothing Oatmeal Bath

To relieve itching from shingles or chicken pox, prepare a hot bath with colloidal oatmeal, and soak in it. You can buy it at any pharmacy or natural-food store.

Diminish Spider Veins

Varicose veins can be diminished by drinking oatstraw tea three times a day. Rubbing bayberry extract on the affected area can relieve the discomfort.

OLIVE
Olea europaea

PERENNIAL

The olive tree has considerable commercial importance in Italy, southern France, Greece and the Middle East, where it has been cultivated for many thousands of years. The many varieties of olive are a result of its having been crossbred and hybridized over the millennia. American cuisine has seen an explosion in the popularity of olive oil over the last fifteen years. While this is partly due to a growing interest in Italian cuisine, it can be accounted for also by America's current interest in healthful foods (olive oil is especially low in saturated cholesterol). Although it is more expensive than other cooking oils, its uniquely sweet richness and its healthful constituents make olive oil a bargain.

In the course of its long history of cultivation, olive oil has found many uses beyond culinary. The ancients used cold-pressed olive oil as an effective laxative, and it is still used in that capacity in some parts of the Middle East. Similarly, the ancients used the oil as a common ingredient in soap, and it can still be found in the list of ingredients in many fine handmade soaps. In North America the olive tree can be cultivated in the more temperate regions and is, in fact, commercially significant in some regions of California.

ONION
Allium cepa

PERENNIAL

This essential kitchen staple is native to central Asia, but having become integral to every major cuisine, it is now cultivated virtually everywhere in the world. We are all familiar with the bulbs of the most popular varieties of onion, since they are readily available at the supermarket. A mature onion plant includes a stalk consisting of five to ten leaves—long, thin and spear shaped. Leaves issue directly from the bulb and grow as high as three feet. The onion is a flowering plant; small purple-white blossoms appear in June and blossom through July.

As with garlic, the ancients ate raw onion. They believed that despite its unpleasant taste, it was a restorer of health and a giver of courage. Also, as with garlic, the ancients were right in one regard. Onion, like garlic, offers the benefit of lowering blood pressure.

Although onion's culinary uses are too various to enumerate, its ornamental potential in the kitchen is sometimes overlooked. Those who grow their own onions have the advantage of pulling their plants whole, drying them, and braiding the leaves to create a "rope" of dried onion, which can be hung as an ornament as used through the winter. Onion is an especially hardy biennial and can easily be sown from seed. Plant these seeds in May, in dark, wet soil, and give it plenty of sun.

OREGANO

Origanum vulgare, Origanum heracleoticum,
Origanum onites

Greek oregano, Italian oregano

     PERENNIAL

This bushy perennial is closely related to marjoram, and some of its many varieties are sometimes understandably mistaken for marjoram. Common

oregano's heart-shaped leaf is larger and broader than the marjoram leaf, and it forms a bushier plant, growing in mounds that are typically one foot high, and two feet across. Oregano flowers in midsummer, bearing inch-long shoots of tiny pink flowers.

In Italy oregano has been a culinary herb since the time of the Romans, and it remains essential to Italian cuisine. Oregano was not introduced to North America until well into the 20th century, but it caught on quickly and is now one of our most commonly used cooking herbs.

While oregano is reputed to have a sedative quality, this has never been documented, and few herbalists continue to use it for this purpose, although it is occasionally used as an antiseptic.

Oregano is easily sown from seed and will thrive in dry soil. It is a good friend to the urban gardener, since it does nicely in a large planter.

OREGON GRAPE

Berberis aquifolium, Mahonia aquifolium

Mountain-berry, holly-leaf barberry

PERENNIAL

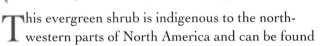

This evergreen shrub is indigenous to the northwestern parts of North America and can be found growing wild from British Columbia to northern California. Its dark green, spiked and leathery leaves give it the common name "holly-leaf barberry." Oregon grape's tiny yellow flower, the state flower of Oregon, appears in midspring and blooms into July. The Oregon grape is not a grape at all, but is a small deep-purple berry. The fruit is edible, but far from sweet.

Oregon grape was introduced to the European settlers by Native Americans. The northwest tribes valued the medicinal properties of its rootstock and used it in a wide variety of ailments. Though it remained popular among folk herbalists throughout the 19th century, its uses today are typically limited to the treatment of dermatological problems.

175

Oregon grape has made a reputation for itself as an excellent landscaping shrub. It makes a perfect free-form hedge, with its dense evergreen leaves. And it will add color to the landscape in both the fall and the spring.

PARSLEY

Petroselinum crispum, Petroselinum sativum

Flat-leaf parsley, curly-leaf parsley

    PERENNIAL

There are three varieties of parsley. All are edible, but it is the flat-leaf and the curly-leaf parsleys that are found in the grocery stores, and in most vegetable gardens. Parsley is indigenous to central Europe, but is now cultivated virtually everywhere in the world.

Parsley is a flowering plant. Under good conditions it will bloom in May or June, bearing very tiny greenish-white florets. In American kitchens parsley tends to be used most as a garnish, but other cultures (and some regional American cuisines) value parsley most for the subtle but distinctive flavor that it lends to sauces and stews. Parsley deserves to be more than an ornament on the plate, since it is loaded with many essential vitamins, including A, C and many of the important B vitamins.

Because it grows dense and low to the ground, parsley makes an excellent border plant in the vegetable or herb garden. Although parsley is a biennial, it sows so easily from seed that it is most commonly treated as an annual. It also makes a very satisfying addition to the herbal planter, since it grows quickly and needs very little attention. Urban apartment dwellers can raise fresh parsley for their kitchens, and indoor winter-planters can bring fresh parsley to the kitchen all year-round.

176

PARTRIDGE

Gaultheria procumbens, Mitchella repens

Partridgeberry

   PERENNIAL

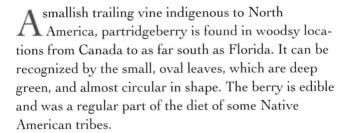

A smallish trailing vine indigenous to North America, partridgeberry is found in woodsy locations from Canada to as far south as Florida. It can be recognized by the small, oval leaves, which are deep green, and almost circular in shape. The berry is edible and was a regular part of the diet of some Native American tribes.

PASSIONFLOWER

Passiflora incarnata

Maypops (fruit)

PERENNIAL

Passionflower has long been used by Native Americans and Europeans alike, as a sedative. Although its safety and efficacy have never been unequivocally demonstrated in the laboratory, most contemporary herbalists will swear by passionflower's mild, narcotic effect. A mild tea can be prepared from dried flowers and young leaves, but amateur herbalists should be aware that large doses will cause nausea and vomiting.

Because passionflower is rather gangly and unsightly before and after its blooming season, it is not a prized garden plant. But it can add an exotic touch to the wildflower garden, with its stunning ten-petaled purple flowers that blossom in May and June. Passionflower is a climbing plant and is especially beautiful running up a trellis in the middle of June. Passionflower also bears a large fruit, called water-lemon by some. The meat of this large berry is seedy, but succulent and sweet.

Sweet Dreams

Herb pillows make a lovely gift and are thought to induce sleep and sweet dreams. Fill a small decorative pillowcase with ground dried hops, German chamomile, lemon verbena leaves, passionflower and sweet woodruff. Make sure the pillow is flat, so it can fit into a pillowcase with a sleeping pillow. Sew the pillow shut.

PENNYROYAL

Mentha pulegium

Pudding grass

  PERENNIAL

Pennyroyal is a member of the mint family and is represented by two varieties. English pennyroyal is now native to this country, while American pennyroyal (sometimes called mock pennyroyal) is indigenous to North America. The American variety is an annual,

Pennyroyal

while the English variety is a perennial. Both varieties resemble the mints, with their opposing, oblong leaves, and square stems. Pennyroyal has a long history as an effective insect repellent. The ancients rubbed it into the skin to protect themselves from fleas and gnats, and Native Americans used the indigenous variety of pennyroyal to ward off mosquitoes and chiggers.

Both the Europeans and the Native Americans found medicinal uses for pennyroyal, but the contemporary herbalist knows that some of its constituents are poisonous. Although some people will drink pennyroyal tea, it should not be taken internally for any reason.

Natural Pet Care

Pennyroyal is an outstanding flea repellent.
Make a liter of pennyroyal tea and rinse your pet
with it once a week for a month. This should
destroy flea eggs. After the bath, rub a mixture
of one tablespoon of pennyroyal oil and one-half
cup of water over your pet's coat. This should
repel fleas. You can also make an herbal flea collar by soaking a regular pet collar in pennyroyal
oil for at least 24 hours. Pennyroyal oil should be
available at your natural-food stores, and at more
progressive pet stores. Caution: Do not use pennyroyal if you are pregnant, or if your pet is
pregnant. It can cause miscarriages.

Pregnant women, especially, should avoid pennyroyal.
Before abortion was legal in this country, pennyroyal
was sometimes used to induce a natural abortion.
While pennyroyal has no use in the kitchen, or as a
medicinal, it still finds a place for itself as an insect
repellent. For this reason it is a practical addition to the
herbal garden. The bushier English variety is a more
pleasing ornamental than the American variety, and
just as effective at repelling insects. To use pennyroyal,
crush the leaves by rolling them firmly between open
palms, then apply the oil to exposed areas of skin.

PEONY
Paeiniae spp.

ANNUAL

This beautiful garden flower is indigenous to China, where it grows wild. It has been introduced to almost every continent on the globe and is native to most regions that will support it. The peony bears beautiful, bushy leaves, surrounding a branching stem that terminates in the flamboyant red, pink or white blossom. Peony flowers in the early spring, and the petals fall back by the end of July. Although the peony root has been traditionally used by Chinese herbalists as a sedative, contemporary herbalists are more likely to turn to other plants when prescribing a tranquilizer. The flowers, however, are still used by many people to make perfumed waters and lotions. The peony is prized by the flower gardener, not only for its striking beauty, but also because it is so easy to care for. Once it is established, it requires little attention, save for occasional watering during dry periods.

Time-Honored Remedy

Many herbs work best externally as healing poultices. Chest congestion and aching joints are two ailments that are greatly soothed by a hot herbal poultice. To prepare an herbal poultice, steep a tablespoon of the herb being used in just-boiled water for ten minutes. Strain the water into a clean glass bowl, and discard the herbs. Dip an unbleached cotton cloth into the herbal water, and apply to affected area.

PEPPER

Piper nigrum

Peppercorn

The coal-colored spice that sits beside the salt shaker on virtually every kitchen table comes to us from a perennial vine that is indigenous to the rain forests of southern India. For centuries it has been cultivated for export to Europe, America, Australia and other parts of Asia.

Always remember that freshly ground cloves or berries are more potent and flavorful than the ground pepper we buy in tins at the supermarket.

PIPSISSEWA

Chimaphila umbellata

Wintergreen, waxflower, princess pine, king's cure, ground holly, love-in-winter, rheumatism weed, ratsbane, dragon's tongue, pyrole

    PERENNIAL

This remedy, native to America, was used by Native Americans and settlers alike to treat rheumatism and induce sweating. As a poultice, it can reduce swelling; ingested as a tea, it will help bring down a fever through sweating. It is also a diuretic and is used by many herbalists to treat cystitis and as a general urinary-tract tonic. It is not a particularly attractive plant, but it makes a fine addition to a medicinal-herb garden. It gives forth pleasant-smelling white flowers, and enjoys sitting in the shade.

PLANTAIN

Plantago major, Plantago lanceolata

English plantain, jackstraw, ribgrass, snake plantain, ribwort, way-bread, Englishman's foot, devil's shoestring, bird seed, snakeweed, ripple grass

PERENNIAL

There are more than a hundred varieties of this common plant. Most of these are characterized by broad base-leaves, which sprout immediately above the roots, and a single rising stem, which terminates in a flowered spike. The most common variety, "white man's foot," grows abundantly throughout most of the United States, just about anywhere the soil is rich and wet. (It has become a scourge in the suburbs, where the keeper of the well-groomed lawn reviles it as a noxious weed.)

Native Americans crushed plantain into a poultice to treat external wounds and sores. Some scientific investigations have shown that it is indeed useful for relieving the itching associated with dermatological inflammation and irritation.

POKEWEED

Phytolacca decandra-americana, Phytolacca americana

Scoke, garget, pigeonberry, crowberry, jalap, pocan bush, inkberry, cancer root, poke sallet

PERENNIAL

This bushy perennial shrub grows in most regions throughout the United States and into Canada. It can be found just about anywhere there is dry, sandy soil and plenty of full sun. Pokeweed will flower in June, bearing tiny white florets, which are followed in autumn by small berries, which ripen to a deep purplish-blue.

Although the Native Americans found some medicinal uses for this plant, it is extremely poisonous and has no place in the kitchen or in the medicine cabinet. Pokeweed's only practical application is as a dyestuff. Herbalists with an interest in dyeing their fabrics by hand know that the ripe pokeweed berry will make a base for a beautiful blue dye.

Apart from this, there is little reason to host pokeweed in your garden. Most gardeners consider it to be an unsightly nuisance.

PUMPKIN

Cucurbita pepo, Cucurbita maxima

Sugar pumpkin, Big Max mammoth pumpkin, Howden pumpkin

ANNUAL

We are all familiar with the many culinary uses for this large bright-orange variety of squash, particularly the integral role that the pumpkin plays on the hallowed eve of All Saints' Day. But European herbalists have long known the pumpkin's singular medicinal application: the seeds, when crushed and dissolved in salt water, make an excellent remedy for tapeworm and other intestinal infestations. It is not an easy cure, however. In order for the solution to work, the patient must fast for at least ten hours before taking it.

PURSLANE

Portulaca oleracea

Pussley

ANNUAL, BIENNIAL

This hearty annual is indigenous to Asia, but has been introduced to many other continents and is now native to most temperate areas of the world. With its reddish-brown branching stem and thick, oblong, succulent leaves, it resembles something like a miniature Joshua tree. It flowers in June, bearing tiny bright-yellow florets.

Purslane is edible and has a pungent, sweet flavor. While it is not commonly eaten in this country, it is a stock vegetable in the diets of many Asian people. In India, especially, purslane is a common ingredient of stews and sauces. While purslane is a fine culinary herb, easy to sow from seed, it must be watched carefully, for it is a fast-spreading ground cover, which can easily overtake other plants.

QUEEN'S DELIGHT

Stillingia sylvatica

Queen's root, silver leaf, yaw root, nettle potato, cock-up-hat, marcony

PERENNIAL

A tincture of this North American native plant was once believed to cure syphilis, but was eventually found to be a better expectorant than an antisyphilitic herb. It is used externally in poultice or ointment form to treat chronic skin problems. Internally, a Queen's Delight tea is an effective laxative and a liver tonic. It is easy to grow in just about any part of North America. It requires only sandy soil and full sun.

RAMP

Allium triccocum

Wild leek

PERENNIAL

The ramp is a wild leek. It appears in the forests and meadows in the early spring and is a delicious, seasonal treat. If you are not an experienced collector of wild plants, do not go off into the woods to find your own ramps. For a brief time in April, many farmers will sell ramps along with their other crops at farmers' markets. Ramps are hard to find, but worth it. They are slightly more pungent than cultivated leeks and can be used in any recipe calling for leeks.

RASPBERRY

Rubus ideas

Brambleberries

PERENNIAL

Raspberries are a delicious summer fruit, used in all kinds of cooking. There is nothing quite so wonderful as a bowl of fresh raspberries with cream for breakfast, or a raspberry tart. Raspberries are used in wines, liqueurs, vinegars, syrups and sauces. The raspberry leaf, however, is an excellent uterine tonic. Many herbalists recommend that pregnant women drink at least one cup of this pleasant-tasting tea every day of their pregnancy. It tones the uterus and helps prepare the body for childbirth. It is also useful in treating female infertility.

ROSE

Rosa damascena (Damask), Rosa gallica (Provence)

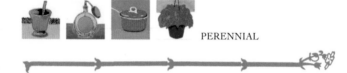

PERENNIAL

There are literally tens of thousands of species of roses. It is perhaps the most popular flowering garden plant in the world. Growing roses takes special care. Be sure to speak with your local nursery to see which rose is right for your garden. Keep in mind that dry, hot weather produces the most fragrant blossoms. Besides its beauty, the rose is a very useful plant. Its oil is used in perfumery and cosmetics, and it is also a natural antiseptic. Rose water is a gentle astringent skin tonic. It is used in pastry baking and to flavor various sweet and savory dishes, especially Middle Eastern and Mediterranean cuisines. Lassi, an Indian yogurt drink, is flavored with rose petals. Rose hips and rose petals make delicious jams and jellies. Most "old" roses, that is, non-hybridized, have medicinal qualities. A syrup made with honey and rose petals is a soothing

High C

Rose hips contain more vitamin C than oranges do. Dried, they make a refreshing and nutritious tea.

sore throat remedy. Rose hips tea has more vitamin C than orange juice. Rose petals are a favorite addition to potpourri. If you are going to prepare your own tea from your garden rose bushes, be sure that you are practicing organic gardening. It is pointless to use rose products that have been doused with harmful pesticides.

ROSEMARY

Rosmarinus officinalis

Tuscan blue, prostratus, alba, creeping rosemary

    PERENNIAL

R osemary is a popular culinary herb, and it is easy to grow. Once a rosemary bush is established in your garden, it will last for years and provide you with fresh, fragrant herbs whenever you need them. It is a

Rosemary Shortbread Cookies

2 sticks unsalted butter
1 cup sugar
3 cups unbleached flour
4 tablespoons fresh rosemary, finely chopped
Dried, crumbled sage

Preheat oven to 300 degrees. Cream the butter and sugar. Add 2½ cups of the flour and mix. Turn out on a floured wooden board, and add the rosemary. Knead the dough until the rosemary is well blended, and the dough does not stick to the board. Roll the dough about ¼ inch thick, and cut into shapes with cookie cutters. Bake on an ungreased cookie sheet for about 35 minutes, or until lightly browned. Sprinkle sage on cookies while still warm. Makes about 30 cookies, depending on your cookie-cutter sizes.

favorite in Mediterranean cuisines and has become popular in regional American cuisine as well. It grows best in full sun with fairly dry soil. It also makes a lovely indoor potherb. It will bloom with delicate blue, pink and white flowers in late spring. These floras are edible and make a lovely garnish or salad topper. In the past, rosemary was used not only to flavor meats, but to preserve them. It has preservative qualities that rival chemical preservatives such as BHA. Rosemary is an essential ingredient in roast leg of lamb. Medicinally, it is a very useful herb. Rosemary tea can be gargles to soothe sore throats. Herbalists prepare a strong infu-

Gourmet Grilling

For an extra infusion of flavor and aroma, crumble a handful of rosemary over coals when you're barbecuing.

sion to relieve headaches, and rosemary ointment is said to alleviate arthritic joint pain. Rosemary tea is also a good digestive tonic. Rosemary is a common ingredient in many dandruff shampoos. Hungary water, an infusion of rosemary and sage, is a wonderful astringent for all complexions. The oil is often used in perfumery.

RUE

Ruta graveolens

Garden rue, herb of grace

PERENNIAL

Rue is a bushy perennial shrub that is native to northern Africa, but is now widely cultivated and has been naturalized to North America. Nearer to the ground, rue's stem is woody, but grows more fleshy toward the top of the shrub. Small ovate leaves are

clustered along minor branchlets, while rue's flower blooms at the terminus of longer branches.

While rue has a 2,000-year history of medicinal applications, contemporary herbalists have only limited uses for it and know that it is toxic when taken in large doses.

Rue has a vaguely weedy look to it, and for that reason, is not often found in the ornamental garden. It is more often cultivated in the herb garden, where it is most appreciated for the unique fragrance it lends to a garden on hot summer days. Rue can be sown from seed, but should be started indoors, in midwinter and planted in early spring. Rue likes dry soil, though not sandy, and requires full sun.

SAFFLOWER
Carthamus tinctorius

False saffron

ANNUAL

Native to northern Africa, safflower has been cultivated in that region and in southern Europe for
thousands of years. Safflower is an annual that typically
grows to two feet in height and bears a bright orange
flower that looks something like a thistle, with spiked
leaves. Safflower's single most useful culinary application is as a cooking oil, for which it has been cultivated
for many thousands of years. Safflower oil is not only
inexpensive, it is very low in saturated cholesterol. In
the flower garden, safflower adds a unique presence,
with its thistle leaves and its bright orange flowers,
which will last through mid-September. Dried thistle is
also an excellent resource for herbal crafts. It will add
a unique texture and color to wreaths and to dried
bouquets. Safflower makes a satisfying addition to the
flower garden, but it prefers temperate climes. Plant it
from seed in dry soil, and be sure that it will get full
sunshine.

Natural Blush

For a natural rouge, mix dried, pulverized saf-
flowers with rice flour or cornstarch.

Combat Male Pattern Baldness

To prevent hair loss, wash your head with an
infusion of sage leaves every day. It's cheaper
than minoxidil!

SAGE

Salvia officinalis, Salvia purpurea, Salvia elegans, Salvia leucantha, Salvia splendens, Salvia clevelandii

Purple sage, variegated sage, pineapple sage, Cleveland sage, meadow sage, true sage, garden sage

     PERENNIAL

There are over 750 varieties of sage grown world-wide, and each has different uses. Some are mainly culinary herbs, others are used medicinally, and others

195

are used as ornamental plants. *Salvia* is most popular in the kitchen and the kitchen garden. It is used to flavor stuffing and many meat dishes. It is baked into breads and cooked with vegetables. Fresh sage leaves are tossed into salads and deep-fried and eaten as a side dish. Pineapple sage *(S. elegans)* is a favorite culinary sage, with a hint of pineapple flavor. It can be used interchangeably with *S. officinalis* in any recipe. *S. purpurea*, purple sage, is also a great culinary herb and is also suitable for use in any recipe calling for garden sage. Sage is often used in commercially prepared soaps and perfumes. It is an astringent and can be found in some facial toners and aftershaves. Sage is wonderful in the kitchen or aromatic garden. It is a natural insect repellent, but will attract bees. Since there are so many varieties of sage, you can choose which colors you like—from the dusty green of Mexican bush sage *(S. leucantha)* to the brightly colored tricolor sage *(S. tricolore)*. Sage is easy to grow. Once it is established, it needs little water and good light. Sage is also a fine potherb. If you have a window herb garden, try planting pineapple sage or dwarf sage. They both do well indoors. The entire plant is edible. Medicinally, sage is thought to be a natural antiperspirant. Some natural-food stores sell deodorants made with sage. Sage is also soothing in tea form to a sore throat. As a mouthwash, it helps clear up mouth and gum problems.

SALAD BURNET

Poterium sanguisorba, Sanguisorba officinalis

Burnet, garden burnet

  PERENNIAL

Salad burnet has been cultivated as a garden herb since at least the 16th century and has been used as a medicinal since before then. It was believed that burnet had blood-clotting properties (it does), thus the Latin name *sanguisorba*. It does have medicinal qualities. Chewing on the leaves helps digestion. Infusions of the whole dried plant are used to treat diarrhea and hemorrhoids. Its astringent qualities make burnet helpful as a poultice in stanching bleeding. Burnet is high in vitamin C, making it a valuable culinary herb. It is delicious in salads. Salad burnet is a good addition to a kitchen garden. It grows nicely in average soils, in temperate climates, but can be grown in the summer just

about anywhere. When it starts to flower, pinch off the blooms to encourage leaf production. Harvest the leaves for salads as you need them, but don't let them grow too large, or they will be bitter.

SANTOLINA

Santolina chamaecyparrisus, Santolina virens

Lavender cotton, Nana, gray santolina, green santolina, dwarf santolina, French lavender

  PERENNIAL

Santolina, or lavender cotton, is a beautiful ornamental plant and a useful aromatic herb. It is rarely used medicinally, but has long been recognized as a valuable moth repellent. It is used in scented sachets for clothes closets and drawers and is a nice addition to homemade potpourri. It blooms in the summer months, with numerous yellow cottonball-shaped flowers and makes an excellent low hedge. It is an evergreen and will grow well in well-drained soil under full sun.

SARSAPARILLA

Smilax aristolochioefolia, Smilax officinalis, Smilax medica, Smilax ornata

Mexican sarsaparilla, hook

 PERENNIAL

Sarsaparilla was another "miracle" herb that the Spaniards brought to Europe from Mexico. The root was used by Mexicans and South Americans to treat syphilis, but was soon discarded when it was realized that it didn't work. Nevertheless, sarsaparilla continued to be used as a treatment for rheumatism, fevers and dermatological disorders until the beginning of the 20th century. It is still used by some folk healers in South America, but contemporary herbalists do not recognize it as a medicinal herb. However, it is used to flavor soft drinks (root beer, sarsaparilla soda) and as a flavoring to mask bitter tastes in commercially prepared medicines. Sarsaparilla tea is a refreshing drink, hot or iced. It grows wild throughout Central and South America and is rarely, if ever, cultivated in North America.

SASSAFRAS

Sassafras officinalis, Sassafras albidum

Ague tree, saxifrax, cinnamon wood, saloop, fennel wood

PERENNIAL

Many herbalists believe that sassafras was the first Native American medicinal plant to reach Europe. It was brought to Spain in the late 16th century and was cultivated in England about the same time. Its essential oil and decoctions of its bark and root were used, until recently, to kill lice. It's also been used as a digestive aid, a stimulant and in a tea to induce sweating. Recent studies have questioned its toxicity, and many herbalists are using other herbs instead of sassafras until more research can be done. The oil is used to flavor tobacco and in making perfume. Sassafras is perhaps best known as the key ingredient in gumbo. *Filé* powder is made from ground dried sassafras leaves. The tree grows wild throughout the central and southern United States. It would make a lovely contribution to a scented garden. It is an aromatic tree, with a scent somewhat reminiscent of fennel and cinnamon, and in the fall the leaves change to brilliant colors.

SAVORY

Satureja hortensis (summer), Satureja montana (winter)

Bean herb, white thyme

ANNUAL, BIENNIAL (WINTER)

Both summer and winter savory are popular culinary herbs and members of the very large mint family. It has been used in kitchens for over 2,000 years. It has been used medicinally as a digestive aid and cough remedy for just as long. Since both summer and winter savories are mints, they are easy to grow. Summer savory is an annual with a slightly milder taste, while winter savory is a hardy perennial with stronger flavors. As cooking seasoning, they are interchangeable. Their warm, slightly sharp taste can be used to season meats, in stuffing and almost anywhere you would use sage or thyme. Both savories make an excellent addition to a kitchen garden and will grow from seed in poor, dry soils.

SAW PALMETTO

Serenoa serrulata, Serenoa repens

Sabal, scrub palm

PERENNIAL

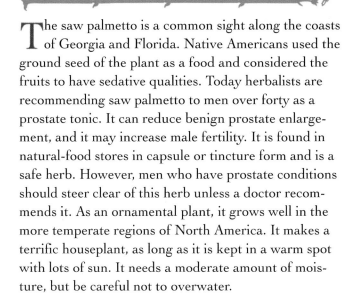

The saw palmetto is a common sight along the coasts of Georgia and Florida. Native Americans used the ground seed of the plant as a food and considered the fruits to have sedative qualities. Today herbalists are recommending saw palmetto to men over forty as a prostate tonic. It can reduce benign prostate enlargement, and it may increase male fertility. It is found in natural-food stores in capsule or tincture form and is a safe herb. However, men who have prostate conditions should steer clear of this herb unless a doctor recommends it. As an ornamental plant, it grows well in the more temperate regions of North America. It makes a terrific houseplant, as long as it is kept in a warm spot with lots of sun. It needs a moderate amount of moisture, but be careful not to overwater.

SCENTED GERANIUM

Pelargonium graveolens

Pink geranium, rose geranium, attar of roses, old spice

PERENNIAL

S cented geraniums, which are no relation to regular geraniums, are called so because of their intoxicating aroma. They are essential in a scented herb garden. Originally from South Africa, these delicate blooms do

well outdoors, with care, in most temperate areas. They make beautiful houseplants and will thrive as long as they are warm enough and get enough sun.

Pelargonium root is used medicinally in parts of Africa as a treatment for diarrhea. It is mainly used in the rest of the world as an ornamental plant. It is widely culti-vated as a commercial crop for its oil, which is used extensively in the men's fragrance industry. It is often substituted for oil of rose. The fresh leaves can be added to cakes, before baking, and to summer salads and fruit dishes. Dried scented geranium leaves are often used in potpourri.

POISON!

These herbs are dangerous, potentially toxic or fatal, and should never be taken internally (although some have benefits as external healing herbs). This list is not all-inclusive, so use cau-tion with any herb unless it is on the Food and Drug Administration's list of herbs that are gen-erally recognized as safe (GRAS):

Aconite	Foxglove
American hellebore	Hemlock
Arnica	Lobelia
Black hellebore	Mandrake
Bloodroot	Mistletoe
Broom	Tansy
Deadly nightshade	Wormwood

Handle With Care

Essential herbal oils are very strong, and usually no more than one drop is necessary for most herbal preparations. They should only be used externally, unless specifically noted.

SELF-HEAL

Prunella vulgaris

Heal-all, brownwort, sicklewort, carpenter's herb, hookweed, wound-wort, blue curls

 PERENNIAL

Self-heal is a weed that grows throughout the Northern Hemisphere. It has long been regarded as a valuable external medicinal herb. It is used topically in a paste or poultice to stop bleeding and as an antiseptic astringent for wounds and cuts. The dried plant can be made into a mouthwash to soothe and treat sore throats and inflammations. It is rarely used internally, except to treat diarrhea, but other herbs work just as well and are safer to use internally. It is rarely grown in the herb garden, since it is, by nature, a weed and will take over much turf.

SENNA

Cassia senna, Cassia acutifolia, Cassia angustifolia.

Locust plant, cassia

PERENNIAL

Senna is a widely used, powerful laxative. It is an ingredient in many commercially prepared over-the-counter laxatives. It is so powerful—can cause cramping and tastes awful—it should only be used as a last resort. There are many other gentler herbal laxatives. It is available in capsule and tincture form. It is rarely recommended as a tea because of its noxious taste. It is not grown in North America.

SESAME

Sesamum indicum, Sesamum montana

Hei Zhi Ma, benne, gingelli

ANNUAL

Sesame is an ancient herb. A native of the tropics worldwide, it is cultivated commercially in Africa, Asia and South America. The seed is the valuable part of the plant. It is expressed for its oil, which is used in cooking and in herbal medicine. The seed and oil are both used as laxatives. The oil can be found in some skin treatments and may be the base for other medicinal preparations prepared with oil. Sesame is best known in the kitchen. The seeds are used in baking and in many Asian and Arabic dishes. The toasted seeds are also made into a zesty oil, especially for cooking. Sesame-seed paste (tahini) is used in numerous Middle Eastern dishes and is a key ingredient in hummus. It is also used to make the confection called halvah.

SHEPHERD'S PURSE

Capsella bursa-pastoris

Shovel weed, Saint-James's-wort, case weed, pick-pocket, mather's heart, clapped pouch, pepper and shot, shepherd's heart, lady's purse, rattle weed

ANNUAL

This European native was introduced to North America by the early colonists and now grows wild throughout North America. It is dried and used internally as a tea to treat bloody urine, nosebleeds, bleeding after childbirth, and heavy menstrual flow. It also contains substances that can induce labor. Shepherd's purse is very bitter tasting. If you use it as a tea, add lots of honey, or mix it with other good-tasting herbs to mask the flavor. It is not known why shepherd's purse stops bleeding, so those with clotting disorders should avoid it. It is a foul-smelling plant and is rarely grown in the garden.

SILVERWEED

Potentilla anserina

Wild tansy

PERENNIAL

Silverweed is a member of the Potentilla family and is a distant cousin of the rose. It is characterized by large silvery leaves with jagged-toothed edges, growing in opposite pairs along a single stem. The buttery-yellow, four-petaled flowers bloom in June atop single, separate stems. Silverweed is not naturalized to North America, but is a common sight in Europe, where it grows wild in wet fields and loamy wasteplaces.

Silverweed has long been considered by European herbalists to be a mild astringent, and a silverweed tea is sometimes prescribed for a sore throat. The herb gardener will appreciate having a small patch of silverweed among her other herbs. Its silver leaves and elegant yellow flowers make a nice contrast to the other colors in the garden.

SKULLCAP

Scutellaria lateriflora

Hoodwort, scute, mad dog, mad weed, Quaker bonnet, blue pimpernel, hooded willow herb, American skullcap

PERENNIAL

This North American native is an excellent sedative. It grows wild anywhere there is moisture or water. The entire plant is used medicinally. It can be dried and ingested as a tea, or as a tincture, can be used before bedtime. It is a weed, but can make an interesting addition to a medicinal garden. It blooms with small blue flowers in the summer and will do well in moist areas with lots of sun.

SLIPPERY ELM

Ulmus fulva, Ulmus rubra

Red elm, moose elm, gray elm

PERENNIAL

Slippery Elm, a North American native tree, grows all over the continent. Its bark was used in a tea by the Ojibwa to treat sore throats and coughs. This practice continues to this day. Slippery Elm bark tea is a pleasant-tasting, soothing throat tonic. Throat lozenges made with slippery elm are readily available in natural-food stores and pharmacies. It is useful as a poultice to soothe wounds. Slippery Elm is a beautiful tree, well worth planting in any garden or yard.

Quit Smoking!

Slippery-elm bark or oatstraw tea can help quell a cigarette craving.

SORREL

Rumex acetosa, Rumex scutatus

French sorrel, common sorrel, sheep sorrel, cuckoo bread, sour dock, sour grass, red weed

     PERENNIAL

Sorrel is used somewhat differently from other herbs. It is a very strong tasting herb because it contains oxalic acid, like spinach and rhubarb. It should be cooked in glass or stainless steel only. This bitter herb is wonderful in cream of sorrel soup or baked into an herb bread. The first sorrel of the spring is tender enough and less acidic, so it can be used, sparingly, in salads, or cooked as a vegetable. Its medinal qualities are minimal, but it does make a wonderful addition to a kitchen garden, and will grow througout the summer until the first frost.

ST.-JOHN'S-WORT

Hypericum perforatum, Hypericum patulatum

PERENNIAL

God's wonderplant, devil's scourge, llamath weed, goat weed, hundred holes, grace of God, herb John, rosin rose, terrestrial sun, amber touch and heal

This European native has been a staple in herbalists cabinets for centuries. It has been used externally in tincture or ointment form to treat bruises and wounds. It is a natural antibacterial herbal treatment. It is taken internally to alleviate menstrual cramps, anxiety and depression, and insomnia. Its powerful antiviral properties have placed it on the list of natural substances being studied for their efficacy at treating AIDS. In the garden, it will grow well in full sun and fairly dry soil. It flowers in the summer months.

Natural Anti-Depressant

Recent studies of Saint-John's-wort show that it may be an effective treatment for mild forms of depression, with fewer side effects.

Middle English Roots

"Wort" is the Middle English word for "herb."

> ### *Allergies Begone!*
>
> Stinging nettle can relieve or stave off an allergy attack. Look for capsules at your natural-food store, and take one capsule every four hours. The tea can prevent acne.

STINGING NETTLE

Urtica dioica, Urtica urens

Common nettle, small nettle, wild nettle, stingers

ANNUAL, PERENNIAL, BIENNIAL

The stinging nettle is a common weed found throughout the eastern United States. It can be recognized by its jagged-edged leaves, growing in opposing pairs, and evenly spaced along the greenish-red stalk. The branching stem of this herb is covered with tiny, hollow needles, which can easily pierce the skin and introduce a painful and irritating toxin to the cuticle nerves.

Nettle hemp has long been used by many cultures to make a variety of fabrics and netting. Native Americans used nettle as a counterirritant, brushing it against those parts of the skin that were inflamed. Native Americans also knew that a poultice made from the leaves is an excellent styptic for minor scrapes and wounds. Pregnant women often drink nettle tea to prepare them for childbirth. Nettle has a long history in Europe as a valued culinary plant.

The young leaves are not only edible, but are quite tasty, and nettle is still an occasional feature in some regional European diets. When it is boiled or sautéed, nettle loses its sting.

If you have young children, you should avoid planting nettle, as its sting is quite painful. If you do plant nettle, and want to introduce it to your kitchen, be sure to wear gloves when you gather or handle it.

STRAWBERRY

Fragaria vesca (wood); Fragaria virginiana (Virginia)

PERENNIAL

Wild strawberry, common strawberry, American strawberry, native strawberry, field strawberry

Strawberries are the first berries of the summer season, They are very fragile and deteriorate rapidly, so local markets are your best bet for freshness and flavor. Buy from local growers. They simply taste better than store-bought berries which may have been shipped across the country. Once you find a strawberry that you like, stock up and freeze or can them. You can use them in all kinds of recipes throughout the year. Strawberries are scrumptious in tarts, jams, ice cream, salsa, etc. In addition to the wonderful things you can do with strawberries in the kitchen, you can make a decoction of the roots and leaves to treat diarrhea. The fruit has a laxative effect. Strawberries are loaded with vitamin C, so if you have a cold, eat lots of them. In the garden, there is nothing quite as satisfying as picking your own strawberries. Go to your local nursery and find the strawberry that is best suited for your soil and climate.

TANSY
Tanacetum vulgare

Bitter buttons, ginger plant, hindheal, English cast, scented fern

  PERENNIAL

Tansy used to be used medicinally, but since it is difficult to measure the amount of thujone, a poisonous alkaloid present in tansy, it is best left to the ornamental garden. This European native has done

> ### *Garden Pest Control*
> Plant tansy and chives in your flower garden to keep aphids away. Marigolds will keep maggots and rabbits at a distance.

well all over North America and will do well in your garden. Its feathery leaves and delicate yellow flowers emit a pinelike scent. It is good to plant tansy in a part of your garden where this lush plant will be brushed against, thus releasing more of the aroma. It needs full sun to partial shade and will grow well in moist or dry soil.

TARRAGON
Artemisia dracunculus, Artemisia sativa

 PERENNIAL

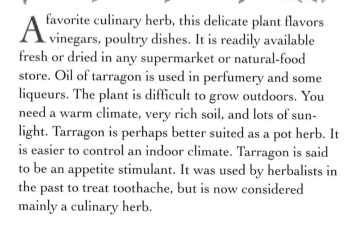

A favorite culinary herb, this delicate plant flavors vinegars, poultry dishes. It is readily available fresh or dried in any supermarket or natural-food store. Oil of tarragon is used in perfumery and some liqueurs. The plant is difficult to grow outdoors. You need a warm climate, very rich soil, and lots of sunlight. Tarragon is perhaps better suited as a pot herb. It is easier to control an indoor climate. Tarragon is said to be an appetite stimulant. It was used by herbalists in the past to treat toothache, but is now considered mainly a culinary herb.

THYME

Thymus vulgaris

French thyme, common thyme

PERENNIAL

Thyme is another herb that few cooks can do without. Keep a pot of thyme growing on your windowsill, so you can have fresh thyme year-round. In addition to its culinary properties, thyme has a place in the herbal medicine cabinet. Its essential oil is a potent

THYME

antiseptic and can be found in many commercially prepared medications. A thyme infusion is a good tonic for
digestive problems and respiratory disorders. The oil is
also used in shampoos and other body cosmetics.
Lemon thyme, one variety of this species, is a popular
culinary herb because of its light lemony overtones. It
can be used whenever thyme is called for in a recipe.
Both thymes grow well in full sun with well-drained
soil. Lemon thyme is an especially nice addition to a
fragrance garden. Its aroma is quite pleasant and
refreshing.

Oven-Fried Herbed Potatoes

8 Purple Peruvian potatoes
Olive-oil spray
1/4 cup chopped fresh thyme
1/4 cup chopped fresh rosemary
1/4 cup olive oil
Salt to taste
Freshly ground pepper to taste

Preheat oven to 375 degrees. Wash potatoes well, and cut into 1/2-inch wedges. Spray a cookie sheet with olive-oil spray, and place the potatoes, skin side down, on the sheet. Drizzle olive oil over potatoes. Sprinkle chopped herbs over potatoes. Season with salt and pepper to taste. Bake for 20 to 30 minutes, or until potatoes are crispy on the outside and soft inside.

Note: You can substitute any fresh kitchen herb for the thyme and rosemary.

UVA URSI

Arctostapholus uva-urse

Bearberry, mountain cranberry, sandberry, bear grape, kinnikinnick, rockberry, crowberry, barren myrtle, universe vine

PERENNIAL

This perennial shrub can be found making a home for itself at high altitudes from Asia to North America. Its wiry branches make a hearty ground cover and will spread even in the driest and sandiest of soils. The tiny white and yellow flowers that this shrub bears in June and July will turn to the red-orange berries in November.

The berries of winter are a staple of the brown bear's diet; hence its name, uva ursi (the bear fruit).

Native Americans knew of many uses for the uva-ursi leaf, including one known to most well-versed herbalists: the tea is reputed to relieve menstrual cramps and pains.

The bearberry bush is a useful agent for the resourceful landscape artist. In places where the soil is too dry to support less hearty plants, this robust ground cover will take root and will make an excellent check against erosion.

VALERIAN
Valeriana officinalis

Garden heliotrope, all-heal, fragrant valerian, phu, setwell, amantilla, nard, cat's love

PERENNIAL

Valerian root is a useful medicinal herb. Known primarily as a sedative, it is often called "natural Valium" because it contains substances that mimic those in Valium. Unlike Valium, it is safe to take valerian when you have been drinking. It is an effective tranquilizer and has been used safely for many years. It was used in World War I to treat shell shock. Valerian root is most readily available in capsule or tincture form at your natural-food store or pharmacy. It tastes and smells awful, so if you decide to make a tea with dried valerian root, you may want to add some other sweet, calming herbs to mask the flavor. Valerian should only be used as needed, and in the recommended dosage. Continued use can result in depression, and an overdose can lead to vomiting and dizziness. The valerian plant is a favorite of ornamental gardeners. There are several varieties that bloom in different colors. Valerian needs full sun and rich moist soil.

VALERIAN

A Literary Herb

Hercule Poirot, Agatha Christie's famous inspector, took valerian drops to help him sleep.

Homemade Gourmet Vinegar

Make your own herbal vinegar. Crush four tablespoons of fresh herbs, and place them in a glass jar. Add one cup of the vinegar of your choice. Cover the jar, and shake well. Let sit for about two weeks, shaking the jar every other day. Check the vinegar's aroma. If the herbal bouquet is not strong enough to your liking, strain the vinegar, remove the herbs, and add fresh ones. When the vinegar is ready, strain the vinegar into a new container. Some excellent combinations for vinegars are tarragon steeped in white-wine vinegar; oregano steeped in red-wine vinegar; cloves and cinnamon steeped in apple-cider vinegar. These vinegars make wonderful gifts. You can put them in ornamental bottles, and add fresh herb sprigs to the vinegar.

VIOLET

Violet odorata

English violet, garden violet, blue violet, sweet violet, heartsease

PERENNIAL

This beautiful, fragrant flowering plant has a well-deserved place in any herb garden. It has been used for thousands of years as an ornamental plant. Its essential oil is one of the first perfumes and is still used widely in perfumery. It flavors many drinks, and the flower can be candied, like ginger. The roots, in tea form, are used medicinally to treat low blood pressure and constipation. The flowers are useful for respiratory disorders. They can be made into a decoction to make a soothing gargle for sore throats. Violets are native to Asia, North Africa and southern Europe. They take

220

great care to grow. They need warm, shady spots with lots of moisture. Talk to your local nursery about which violets are best for your particular area.

WAHOO

Euonymus atropurpureus

Burning bush, arrow wood, spindle tree, skewer wood

PERENNIAL

Wahoo is an American native plant and was used in a poultice by Native Americans to treat facial sores. They also used it internally as a diuretic and stimulant. Often the wood from the small shrub would be used to make pipe stems and arrow shafts. However, wahoo is quite toxic, and its use as a medicinal plant has fallen out of favor. Wahoo will grow anywhere, in any soil. It is not particularly attractive, but is of historic interest. It would enhance a native-plant garden.

WATERCRESS

Nasturtium officinale, Radicula nasturtium-aquaticum

Sisymbrium

PERENNIAL

Watercress is a common herb, growing wild just about everywhere. It is a wonderful salad herb, and can be used in soups and sauces. No tea party would be complete without watercress sandwiches. It is also a valuable and nutritious medicinal herb. It is

high in vitamins A, B₂, C, D, and E. It contains essential minerals such as manganese, iron, calcium and phosphorus. Watercress is an effective diuretic and will also soothe an upset stomach. Its antiseptic qualities make it soothing cough remedy when mixed with honey. Some folk herbalists believe it to be an aphrodisiac, but there is only anecdotal evidence to back up that particular claim. It is easy to grow in your garden. Just give it lots of water, and it will grow like a weed, which, in fact, it really is.

WILD CARROT

Daucus carota

Queen Anne's lace

BIENNIAL

The wild carrot is a European native, but this plant has become a familiar sight along highways all over the world. The distinctive white flowers, with the tiny purple single bloom in the center, are favorites to gather in the summer. Wild carrot and its domesticated relatives are all good sources of vitamin A, the B vitamins, vitamin C and potassium. The roots are edible and nutritious. Dried wild-carrot root is used medicinally to treat urinary-tract problems, and the juice can help alleviate acid stomach. It is mostly a wild plant, but gardeners who are cultivating a "wild" garden find Queen Anne's lace to be a lovely addition.

WILD YAM

Dioscorea spp.

Colic root, China root, devil's bones, rheumatism root, Chinese yam, bitter yam

PERENNIAL

There are over 200 species of yams that grow in tropical to temperate climates. Although they are tubers, they are not related to the sweet potato, which is a member of the Morning Glory family. Some species are used for food, and others are used medicinally. *D. villosa* is native to North America, and well over 100 are native to Mexico and South America. The dried rhizome is used to treat morning sickness and colic. Some herbalists believe that the wild-yam can help prevent miscarriage. Many women today use wild-yam cream externally to alleviate the symptoms of premenstrual syndrome and menopause. Yam is easy to grow. Find an edible species, and plant it near a wall. The leaves will climb gracefully, and you can dig up the tubers as you need them.

WINTERGREEN
Gaultheria procumbens

Teaberry, boxberry, partridgeberry, checkerberry, pigeon berry, clink, tea of Canada

PERENNIAL

This small evergreen is native to North America and grows all over the continent. It is a favorite medicinal tea among herbalists and is used to treat chronic diarrhea. It is a mild stimulant and is said to increase milk production in nursing mothers. Topically, oil of wintergreen is often used to treat body aches. It contains methyl salycilate, which is closely related to aspirin. Oil of wintergreen is used in soaps, cleansers, mouthwashes and facial toners. It has a minty-sweet flavor, which lends taste to candies and chewing gums. It is a rejuvenating scent often used in aromatherapy. The wintergreen plant grows well in North America, best in sandy soils in partial shade. It blooms with small white and red flowers and gives forth a small, edible fruit, which is a favorite among wild animals and some people.

WITCH HAZEL

Hamamelis virginiana

Snapping hazel, spotted alder, winterbloom, striped alder

Witch hazel has been a valuable herbal medicine for centuries. Native to North America, it was used by Native Americans to disinfect and heal cuts, bruises, insect bites, boils and other skin ailments. They also used it internally as a tea to treat fevers, prevent miscarriage, and soothe sore throats. The European colonists soon adopted the native use of witch hazel, and it has remained a valuable medicinal ever since. Today it is used primarily as an external application or gargle. Drinking witch-hazel tea is not encouraged. A decoction or distillation of the bark is readily available in supermarkets, natural-food stores and corner stores. It is a cooling astringent and antiseptic. It is used in facial toners and commercial hemorrhoid medicines. As an ornamental plant, it is a colorful contribution to a garden. It loses its leaves each fall, but gives forth yellow flowers well into the late fall. It grows best in moist soils in partial shade, but is adaptable to almost any garden environment, except a completely arid one.

Cool Your Jets

During the hot summer months, keep a bottle of witch hazel in your refrigerator. For a cooling pick-me-up, soak a cotton ball with the chilled witch hazel, and rub over your face and neck.

WOAD

Isatis tinctoria

Dyer's weed

BIENNIAL

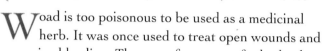

Woad is too poisonous to be used as a medicinal herb. It was once used to treat open wounds and excessive bleeding. There are far more safer herbs than woad, however, that perform the same function. It is

now planted primarily as an ornamental herb. It blooms with beautiful yellow flowers and deep purple seedpods. It does best in full sun in well-drained soil. Before indigo was imported from the Far East, Europeans used woad leaves to create blue dyes. Today it is rarely used as a dye, but those with an interest in herbal dyes may wish to experiment with woad. Ancient Britons painted their bodies blue with paste made from woad before they went into battle.

WORMWOOD

Artemisia absinthium

Absinthe, madderwort, mingwort

PERENNIAL

This notorious European plant was used medicinally to kill intestinal parasites. Unfortunately, this treatment often killed the host as well. Wormwood is a highly toxic plant and should never be used in a home herbal treatment. It is the key ingredient in absinthe, an aperitif that was considerably popular in the 19th century. This liquor is banned in most countries today. It was an addictive, but dangerous, pleasure of many 19th-century writers and painters. The active chemical in wormwood—thujone—can cause nightmares, hallucinations, insomnia, convulsions, vomiting and finally death. Large amounts of wormwood can cause permanent damage to the central nervous system. Some art historians believe that it was Vincent Van Gogh's addiction to absinthe that drove him mad and eventually to suicide. In spite of all these caveats, wormwood is used to flavor other liquors, such as vermouth and Campari. The amount used is so small it is not dangerous, and it imparts a desired bitterness to the drink. Wormwood is an effective moth and flea repellent. It is also used

externally as a medicinal herb. Compresses soaked in
wormwood tea alleviate the pain of bruises and
sprains. It has antiseptic qualities and is used in some
commercially prepared antiseptics. In the garden,
wormwood is quite attractive. Its grayish-green leaves
make attractive bedding, and it will grow in even the
worst soil. Be careful where you plant it, though. It can
kill other plants.

YARROW

Achillea millefolium

Milfoil, thousand-leaf, bloodwort, staunchgrass, nosebleed, soldier's woundwort, saguinary, old man's pepper, devil's plaything, carpenter's weed

    PERENNIAL

Since ancient times yarrow has been associated with healing wounds and stopping bleeding. Achilles was said to have treated his injured soldiers with

yarrow, thus the name *achillea*. Native Americans used yarrow externally to treat wounds, cuts, burns and bruises. Yarrow is no longer used to treat soldiers' wounds, but it has many other uses. Yarrow tea is thought to regulate menstrual periods. It also lessens the symptoms of premenstrual syndrome, since it is a mild sedative and an anti-inflammatory. Dried yarrow is mixed with elderflowers and peppermint to make a soothing tea for colds. It is often found in skin-care products formulated for oily skin, and in hair-care products. It has been known as a cleanser for light-colored hair since prehistoric times.

Though native to Europe, yarrow has spread over the globe. It will grow just about anywhere, in sunlight and shade, and is drought resistant. Its pink or white flowers and aromatic foliage make an attractive and hardy addition to an herb garden.

YELLOW DOCK

Rumex crispus

Rumex, curled dock, narrow-leafed dock, bitter dock, sour dock, out-sting, dock root

PERENNIAL

Yellow dock, a European native, grows wild throughout both hemispheres. It blooms in the summer and is a member of the buckwheat family. It is not a garden herb, nor is it used in cooking, but it does have some medicinal properties. It was a favorite herb of Native Americans and early colonists. The dried root has been used in a decoction by herbalists to treat anemia. It is also a laxative, and the powdered root is helpful in treating gingivitis. The leaves were once used to treat scurvy, since they are high in vitamin C, but they are also high in oxalic acid, which can be toxic in high concentrations. Thus, the practice of using yellow-dock leaves has ceased. As a poultice, rumex is useful in treating skin eruptions.

YELLOW PARILLA

Menispermum canadense

Canadian moonseed, vine-maple, Texas sarsaparilla, yellow sarsa-parilla

PERENNIAL

Yellow parilla grows wild throughout North America, and thrives in moist soils. It gives forth small yellow flowers in the summer, and a grapelike fruit. The root is sometimes used as a substitute for sarsaparilla. In the past it was used by herbalists in a tea to treat blood disorders and immunity problems. A tincture of yellow parilla root may still be useful in alleviating backaches and headaches. Be warned—it has a fairly bitter taste. There are many other analgesic herbs that have a more pleasing favor. Yellow parilla is perhaps best used as an ornamental herb.

YERBA SANTA

Eriodictyon californicum

Mountain balm, consumptive's weed, gum bush, bear's weed, holy herb, tarweed

PERENNIAL

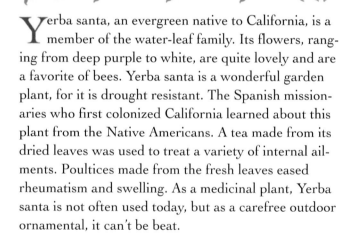

Yerba santa, an evergreen native to California, is a member of the water-leaf family. Its flowers, ranging from deep purple to white, are quite lovely and are a favorite of bees. Yerba santa is a wonderful garden plant, for it is drought resistant. The Spanish missionaries who first colonized California learned about this plant from the Native Americans. A tea made from its dried leaves was used to treat a variety of internal ailments. Poultices made from the fresh leaves eased rheumatism and swelling. As a medicinal plant, Yerba santa is not often used today, but as a carefree outdoor ornamental, it can't be beat.

YEW

Taxus baccata

PERENNIAL

A few years ago the graceful yew tree, a Pacific Northwest native, received quite a bit of publicity. Researchers for a major drug company found that an extract of its bark showed great promise in treating ovarian cancer, and they developed a drug called taxol. However, the yew tree is an endangered evergreen species. Environmentalists were caught in a Hobson's choice of whether to protest the harvesting of yew bark from the few remaining yew forests, or to support what was, at the time, the most exciting experimental breast-cancer drug to ever have been developed. Fortunately, chemists were able to synthesize taxol, and the problem of the yews resolved itself. The trees still stand in Washington and Oregon. You can plant one in your yard, if you live in a moderate, moist climate.

YOHIMBÉ

Corynanthe yohimbe, Pausinystalia yohimba

Yohimbine

PERENNIAL

The Yohimbé is a tree that grows in tropical West Africa. Its bark is one of the world's most popular aphrodisiacs for men, although there is little evidence to uphold its reputation. Nevertheless, you will find it in many natural-food stores in capsule or extract form. In very large doses, it does cause dilation of the blood vessels, which might result in an erection. Men with low blood pressure should never use yohimbine, and others should consider that the effective dose is almost toxic. It is also a monoamine oxidase (MAO) inhibitor. If you are taking yohimbé, you should avoid all foods containing the amino acid tyrosine—red wine, beer, cheese, chocolate, smoked meats and fish, anything fermented, etc., and any antihistamines or decongestants. The combination can be fatal. Anecdotal evidence suggests that yohimbé may do more harm than good—one man experienced dizziness and stomach cramps after using a tincture of yohimbé bark. Another fellow experienced extreme anxiety attacks. Should you use yohimbine? The choice is yours, but there are safer aphrodisiacs.

ZATAR

Thymbra spicata

 PERENNIAL

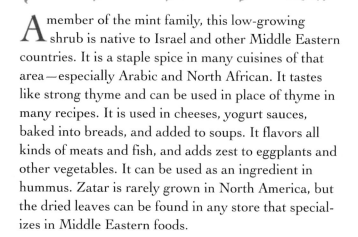

A member of the mint family, this low-growing shrub is native to Israel and other Middle Eastern countries. It is a staple spice in many cuisines of that area—especially Arabic and North African. It tastes like strong thyme and can be used in place of thyme in many recipes. It is used in cheeses, yogurt sauces, baked into breads, and added to soups. It flavors all kinds of meats and fish, and adds zest to eggplants and other vegetables. It can be used as an ingredient in hummus. Zatar is rarely grown in North America, but the dried leaves can be found in any store that specializes in Middle Eastern foods.

MAIL ORDER SOURCES
for Herbs and Herbal Products

Dried Herbs

BENNETT VALLEY FARM
6797 Giovanetti Road
Forestville, California 95436
707-887-9557

Dried herbs and flowers, garlic

CHAMISE CREEK COUNTRY GARDENS
14937 Chamise Creek Road
Ramona, California 92065
619-789-8940

Dried herbs and everlastings, potted herbs, herbal products, gifts

GABRIEANA'S
P.O. Box 215322
Sacramento, California 95821
800-684-4372

Dried herbs, cosmetics, essential oils, teas, herb-crafting supplies

MEADOWS DIRECT
13805 Highway 136
Onslow, Iowa 52321
319-485-2723
800-542-9771

Dried roses

PARK AVENUE HERBAL SHOPPE
3020 Park Avenue
Memphis, Tennessee 38114
Bulk medicinal herbs

RASLAND FARMS
Route 1, Box 65 C
Godwin, North Carolina 28344-09712
910-567-2705
Culinary herbs, teas, dried flowers, herbal gifts

SAN FRANCISCO HERB CO.
250 14th Street
San Francisco, California 94103
800-227-4530
Organic dried herbs, potpourris and oils

VINTAGE HERBS
9753 Green Valley Road
Sebastopol, California 95472
707-823-7100
Dried herbs and flowers, plants
Herb-Crafting and Herb-Crafting Supplies

ESSENTIALS AND SUCH
4746 W. Jennifer Avenue, Suite 107
Fresno, CA 93722-9755
209-277-4747
209-277-9755 (FAX)
Email: EnSuch@aol.com
Bottles, jars, vials, caps, corks, droppers, seals, netting, melt tanks,
waxes, salts, bar soap bases, dilutants, dispersants, etc.

JOPLA ENTERPRISES
P.O. Box 621655
Littleton, Colorado 80162
303-979-9265
303-972-6792 (FAX)
Spanish-glass bottles

LAVENDER LANE
7337 #1 Roseville Road
Sacramento, California 95842
916-334-4400
916-339-0842 (FAX)
Hard-to-find herbal ware

SOAP SALOON
7309 Sage Oak Court
Citrus Heights, California 95621
916-723-6859

Soap and candlemaking supplies, bath products

SUNBURST BOTTLE COMPANY
7001 Sunburst Way
Citrus Heights, California 95621
916-722-4632

Complete herb-crafting supplies

VIREO COUNTRY GOODS
100 ½ Main Street
Delhi, New York 13753
607-746-7277

Handmade, hand-painted herb-drying racks

Herb Plants

AKIN' BACK FARM
2501 Highway 53 South
LaGrange, Kentucky 40031
502-222-5791

Herb plants, perennials, everlastings

BROWN'S EDGEWOOD GARDENS
2611 Corrine Drive
Orlando, Florida 32803
407-896-3203

Annuals and perennials, organic gardening products

COUNTRY FLOWERS
P.O. Box 10
Napanoch, NY 12458
914-647-5256
914-647-3794 (FAX)

250 varieties of herbs

DRAGONFLY FARM
425 Westside Road
Healdsburg, California 95448
707-433-3739

Herbs, field-grown flowers, ornamentals

DUTCH MILL HERB FARM
6640 NW Marsh Road
Forest Grove, Oregon 97116

Specializes in lavenders

FROG POND ORGANIC FARM
5300 Stoney Ridge Road
Campbell, NY 14821
607-527-3308
Organically grown herb plants

GREENFIELD HERB GARDEN
Depot & Harrison, P.O. Box 9
Shipshewana, Indiana 46565
Herb plants

THE HERB GARDEN
P.O. Box 773
Pilot Mountain, NC 27041
400 varieties of herbs

LINDA'S GARDEN
17262 Bodega Highway
Bodega, California 94922
707-876-3466
Herb plants, handcrafted soaps

LOGEE'S GREENHOUSE
141 North Street
Danielson, Connecticut 06239
860-774-8038
Herbal plants

MOM'S HEAD GARDENS
4153 Langner Avenue
Santa Rosa, California 95407
707-585-8575
Organic medicinal-herb plants, fresh and dried herbs

NICHOLS GARDEN NURSERY
1190 S. Pacific
Albany, Oregon 97321
503-928-9280
Herbs, vegetables, flowers

OCEAN SONG FARM AND WILDERNESS CENTER
19100 Coleman Valley Road
P.O. Box 659
Occidental, California 95465
707-874-2442
Herbs, flowers; 240-acre nature preserve

PENNY'S GARDEN
P.O. Box 305
Blacks Creek Road
Mountain City, Georgia 30562
706-746-6918

Herb plants, scented geraniums, garden accessories, dried arrangements

RASLAND FARM
Rt. 1, Box 65
Godwin, NC 28344
910-567-2705

Culinary-herb plants, dried herbs, teas

THE ROSEMARY HOUSE AND GARDEN
120 South Market Street
Mechanicsburg, PA 17055
717-697-5111

Herb plants, scented geraniums, saffron bulbs

STORY HOUSE HERB FARM
Route 7, Box 246
Murray, Kentucky 42071
502-753-4158

Organically grown herb plants

SUNNY ACRES HERB FARM
P.O. Box 249
Dayton, TX 77535
409-258-5129

Plants, books, gifts, garden accessories

TOMASINI GARDENS
217 Fair Avenue
Petaluma, California 94952
707-765-0880

Culinary herb plants

VILLAGE ARBORS
1804 Saugahatchee Road
Auburn, Alabama 36830
334-826-3490
800-288-5033
334-821-0482 (FAX)

Herb plants

WELL-SWEEP HERB FARM
317 Mt. Bethel Road
Port Murray, NJ 07865
908-852-5390
Medicinal plants, herb plants

WOODSIDE GARDENS
1191 Egg & I Road
Chimacum, Washington 98325
360-732-4754
Heirloom herbs and new cultivars

WRENWOOD
Rt. 4, Box 361
Berkeley Springs, West Virginia 25411
304-258-3071
Herb plants, scented geraniums

YA-KA-AMA NATIVE PLANT NURSERY
Ya-ka-ama Indian Education and Development, Inc.
6215 Eastside Road
Forestville, California 95436
707-887-1586
Native plants, trees, ornamental grasses
Herb Seeds

AMERICAN SEED CORPORATION
58233 Gratiot Avenue
New Haven, Connecticut 48048
Seed catalogue

BURPEE
Warminster, Pennsylvania 18974
215-674-1793
Seed catalogue; gardening accessories

EPICURE SEEDS, LTD.
Avon, New York 14414
Culinary seeds, specialty seeds

FARMER SEED AND NURSERY COMPANY
Faribault, Minnesota 55021
Seed catalogue

THE FLOWERY BRANCH
P.O. Box 1330
Flowery Branch, Georgia 30542
1,500 varieties of seeds for culinary, ornamental and medicinal herbs and dye plants

GOODWIN CREEK GARDENS
P.O. Box 83
Williams, Oregon 97544
503-846-7357

Plants and seeds for 500 herbs — rare lavenders, Native American herbs

HEIRLOOM GARDENS
Dept. A, P.O. Box 5277
Lancaster, PA 17606-5277

Antique varieties of herbs — seeds and plants

THE HERBFARM
Tray 8A
32804 Iss.-Fall City Road
Fall City, Washington 98024
800-866-4372
206-789-2279 (FAX)

Herbal products — cosmetics and skin care, teas, vinegars, books, videos, seeds

MELLINGER'S
2344DL Range Road
North Lima, Ohio 44452-9731

Herb seeds, herb plants, gardening items

NICHOLS GARDEN NURSERY
1190 South Pacific
Albany, Oregon 97321
503-928-9280

Plants and seeds

REDDING'S COUNTRY CABIN
13150 E. US Highway 421
Ronda, North Carolina 286709
800-462-2451

Herb plants, seeds, scented geraniums, eucalyptus, herbal extracts, essential oils, dried herbs

THE SANDY MUSH HERB NURSERY
316 Surrett Cove Road
Leicester, North Carolina 28748-9622

Herb seeds, scented geraniums, 1,300 herbs, garden plants

SEED SAVERS EXCHANGE
R.R. 2
Princeton, Missouri 64673

Seed exchange, rare seeds

SELECT SEEDS ANTIQUE FLOWERS
180 Stickney Hill Road
Union, Connecticut 06076

Vintage seeds, ornamental herbs

SHEPARD'S GARDEN SEEDS
30 Irene Street
Torrington, CT 06790

Herb seeds, heirloom fruits and vegetables, edible flowers

SHEPARD'S GARDEN SEEDS
6116 Highway 9
Felton, California 95018
408-335-6910

Specialty seeds

THE THYME GARDEN
Herb Seed Company
20546 Alsea Highway
Alsea, Oregon 97324
503-487-8671

Specialty seeds, plants, hops, ginseng, dried herbs, teas

TINMOUTH CHANNEL FARM
Box 428 B
Tinmouth, VT 05773
802-446-2812

Herb plants and seeds; no shipping to California, Oregon, Washington or Canada

WESTVIEW HERB FARM
P.O. Box 3462
Poughkeepsie, NY 12603
914-462-3534

Herb seeds, medicinal herbs, culinary herbs
Herbal Products

AROMALAND, INC.
800-933-5267

Essential oils, aromalamps, aroma accessories

AROMATHERAPY INTERNATIONAL
300 N. Fifth Street, Suite 210
Ann Arbor, Michigan 48104
313-741-1617
313-741-7109 (FAX)

Essential oils, floral waters, cosmetics

THE ESSENTIAL OIL COMPANY
P.O. Box 206
Lake Oswego, Oregon 97034
800-729-5912

Essential oils, aromatherapy supplies, potpourri and fragrance oils, incense materials

FRAGRANT EARTH COMPANY
544 Saville Crescent
North Vancouver V7N 3B1 Canada
604-983-3401
604-732-6013 (FAX)

Essential oils

HERBAL INDULGENCE
300 Queen Anne Avenue North, Suite 378
Seattle, WA 98109
800-782-4532 or
206-282-4532
Email:samarabotane@wingedseed.com
WWW http://wingedseed.com/samara/

Essential oils, herbal preparations and cosmetics

HILLSIDE HERBS AROMATIC JEWELRY
1710 Allied Street, Suite 35
Charlottesville, Virginia 22903
804-295-5547

Naturally scented herb beads, aromatherapy and jewelry

JAY DESIGN
365 N. Craig Street
Pittsburgh, Pennsylvania 15213
412-683-1184

Handmade bath and cosmetic soaps

LAKON HERBALS

RR 1, BOX 4710 TEMPLETON ROAD
Montpelier, Vermont 05602
802-223-5563

Herbal massage oils, salves, creams

LUNAR FARMS HERBAL SPECIALISTS
3 Highland – Greenhills
Gilmer, Texas
800-687-1052

Bath salts, body and massage oils

NATIVE ESSENSE HERB COMPANY
216 M North Pueblo, #301
Taos, New Mexico 87571
800-358-0513

Herbal extracts and formulas, hard-to-find Native American herbs

SONOMA WREATH AND HERB COMPANY
979 Chiquita Road
Healdsburg, California 95448
800-807-7673
707-433-5345 (FAX)

Herbal wreaths, herbal-champagne vinegars

SUN FEATHER HERBAL SOAP COMPANY
800-771-7627
315-265-2902 (FAX)

Herbal soaps, shampoos and candles; soap-making supplies

WILD SAGE
P.O. Box 631
Lyons, Colorado 80540

Skin-care products

Medicinals

AMERICA'S FINEST, INC.
800-350-3305

Nutritional supplements

THE AROMATHERAPY STORE
117 N. Robertson Boulevard
Los Angeles, California 90048
800-677-2368

Organic essential oils; aromatherapy classes

CARE RESOURCES
3500 Stanley Avenue
North Las Vegas, Nevada 89030
702-642-9261

Medicinal-herb seeds

ELIXIR FARM BOTANICALS
Brixey, Missouri 65618
417-261-2393

Chinese and Native American medicinal plants and seeds

FLORA LABORATORIES
50 Warner Road
Trout Lake, Washington 98650
800-395-6093
Organically grown herbal and homeopathic remedies

MOONRISE HERBS
1068 ìlî Street
Arcata, California 95521
800-603-8364
707-822-0506 (FAX)
Organic herbs, tincture, salves

NATIVE ESSENSE HERB COMPANY
216 M North Pueblo, #301
Taos, New Mexico 87571
800-358-0513

Resources and Associations

AMERICAN BOTANICAL COUNCIL
P.O. Box 201660
Austin, Texas 78720
Information and research services

HERB GATHERINGS 2000
10949 East 200 South
Lafayette, Indiana 47905-9453
317-296-4116
National herb organization

**HERB GROWING AND MARKETING
NETWORK (HGMN)**
P.O. Box 245
Silver Spring, Pennsylvania 17575-0245
717-393-3295
Computer bulletin board (HerbNet)

HERB RESEARCH FOUNDATION
1007 Pearl Street, Suite 200
Boulder, Colorado 80302
303-449-2265
303-449-7849 (FAX)
Information and research services

THE HERB SOCIETY OF AMERICA
9019 Kirtland Chardon Road
Kirtland, OH 44094
216-256-0514
216-256-0541 (FAX)

Quarterly newsletter, seed exchange, lending privileges to a 1,000-volume herbal library

INTERNATIONAL HERB ASSOCIATION
1202 Allanson Road
Mundelein, Illinois 60060
708-949-4372
708-566-4580 (FAX)

Herbal professionals' organization; publishes Today's Garden

UNITED PLANT SAVERS
P.O. Box 420
East Barre, Vermont 05649

Bioregional information about threatened and endangered plants; seed resources